Zed Books is an independent progressive publisher with a reputation for cutting-edge international publishing. Innovative and thought-provoking, the **Economic Controversies** series strips back the often impenetrable façade of economic jargon to present bold new ways of looking at pressing issues, while explaining the hidden mechanics behind them. Concise and accessible, the books bring a fresh, unorthodox approach to a variety of controversial subjects.

Already published in the Economic Controversies series:

Yanis Varoufakis, *The Global Minotaur: America, the True Origins of the Financial Crisis and the Future of the World Economy*

About the authors

Robert R. Locke is Emeritus Professor at the University of Hawaii at Manoa. He is one of the leading international authorities on the contentious subject of management, and the author of numerous books and articles on comparative management and management education.

J.-C. Spender is Visiting Professor at Lund University's School of Economics and Management and at ESADE (Universitat Ramon Llull). Now retired after seven years as a business school dean, he works as a consultant, researcher, writer, lecturer, and generally itinerant academic.

Confronting Managerialism

How the Business Elite and Their Schools Threw Our Lives Out of Balance

Robert R. Locke and J.-C. Spender

Zed Books
London & New York

Confronting Managerialism: How the Business Elite and Their Schools Threw Our Lives Out of Balance was first published in 2011 by Zed Books Ltd, 7 Cynthia Street, London N1 9JF, UK and Room 400, 175 Fifth Avenue, New York, NY 10010, USA

www.zedbooks.co.uk

Typeset in Bulmer MT
by Bookcraft Ltd, Stroud, Gloucestershire
Index by Rohan Bolton,
Rohan.Indexing@gmail.com
Cover designed by www.alice-marwick.co.uk

A catalogue record for this book is available from the British Library
Library of Congress Cataloging in Publication Data available

ISBN 978 1 78032 072 4 hb
ISBN 978 1 78032 071 7 pb

To the many victims of managerialism

"The owl of Minerva takes flight at dusk."
– *G. F. W. Hegel*

Contents

Tables and figure

Tables

Figure

Acknowledgments

We would like to thank Edward Fullbrook, general editor of the Zed Books series Economic Controversies, for rousing us from our dogmatic slumbers with a request to write this short book on managerialism and business schools. We acknowledge, too, our debt to the following colleagues for their splendid help in the preparation of the text and the manuscript: Kenneth A. Locke, Chair of the Department of Religious Studies, University of the West, for material about Christianity; David A. Carter, Associate Professor of Finance, Oklahoma State University, Stillwater, for information on finance; and Vanessa Karam, of University of the West, and Idus A. Newby, of Cochran, Georgia, for their prompt and skillful editing of the manuscript. The final result, of course, is solely our responsibility.

RRL
JCS

Preface

As historians, we are keenly aware that our focus is on the thoughts and actions of the three generations who lived through the period covered in this study – from the Great Depression of the 1930s to the present. But we also know that "dumb" facts do not speak for themselves, and that to give them a voice we need a narrative line. Ours can be identified from the components of our title, and it is simple. Today the people of the USA, indeed the world, live in difficult times, and to a significant extent American managerialism and US business schools have exacerbated these difficulties. Their ideas and actions shape the US and world economies and thus many lives.

Notice our title deals with managerialism, not management. Management is a big topic that cannot be properly treated here. Our focus is narrower, on managerialism. Although by the middle of the twentieth century the American idea of management had been more or less subsumed by managerialism, management and managerialism are not coextensive. While management can be defined as getting things done in organizations through people, managerialism means that in businesses, managers have come to view themselves as a professional caste.

The distinction between managing and managerialism allows us to criticize managerialism without denigrating the critically important function of management.

Managerialism is defined as follows:

> What occurs when a special group, called management, ensconces itself systemically in an organization and deprives owners and employees of their decision-making power (including the distribution of emoluments) – and justifies that takeover on the grounds of the managing group's education and exclusive possession of the codified bodies of knowledge and know-how necessary to the efficient running of the organization. (Locke, 2009, 28)

The managerialist caste arose in the mid-twentieth century as the post–World War Two economy boomed. Its public face was the reputation for commercial brilliance the boom implied. Yet the connection is far from obvious; many other causes can be cited. So, far from presuming the changes in management technique and attitude were beneficial, our book examines the damaging impacts this caste and its practices had in other ways, for instance, on people's ability to make sense of their existence in a globalized society and economy as the twentieth century drew to a close. Without wishing to evoke a previous "golden age," our narrative line moves from managing in a place where life was relatively in balance to one in which, in part because of the effect of managerialism, life spun progressively out of balance. The expression is taken from the Hopi word *Koyaanisquatsi*, which means "crazy life, life in turmoil, life out of balance, life disintegrating, a state of life that calls for another way of living." Or, for those with religious inclinations, an existence without God's grace; or, for humanists, one devoid of humanity in people's daily lives.

With the history of managerialism as one theme, our book's companion topic is business school education. Managers get their education in a variety of ways today, usually on the job. Increasingly, however, the selection and training of managers has become the focus of business-school-based education. Thus we critique the US elite business schools whose growth in the twentieth century has been associated with the rise of managerialism (Locke 1984, 1989, 1996, 2000, 2009; Spender 2005, 2007, 2008a, 2008b, 2008c). The elite schools' influence over the lesser-ranked schools around the world is huge, especially when it comes to the content of their programs and the ethos their programs inculcate. The management education industry is now vast and global, but almost all of it marches to these elite schools' drummers. Harvard Business School, which opened in 1908, has just celebrated its centennial while the Wharton School, arguably the first modern US business school, dates to 1881 (Engwall and Zamagni, 1998; Sass, 1982). Many other business schools – Chicago, Dartmouth, Columbia, University of Texas, etc. – trace their origins to the first quarter of the twentieth century. However, business school growth really exploded after World War Two with the proliferation of Master of Business Administration (MBA) programs driven, in part, by the GI Bill's support for the broad expansion of higher education and in part by the needs of a dynamic economy. The schools' growth has continued, even as the US economy has faltered from time to time. Business studies now preoccupy one of every five US college students. Eventually US business education, along with US systems of corporate governance and finance, became major export items.

While concerned with the form and content of business school education, our book is not a further addition to the expanding literature charging business schools with failing to deliver against their original promise (Khurana, 2007). We are preoccupied, rather, with how that promise never meshed well with the US's – and the wider world's – management needs, and instead helped progressively to spin our lives out of balance. Management is a practice; hence, business studies, like other practitioner disciplines, must stand on intimate acquaintance with the context of the practice it purports to teach. The subtleties of the interactions between theorists and experimenters in the natural sciences show that this intimacy does not necessarily mean that business theorists have to engage in business themselves. But they do need to remain attached to the world of business practice and resist the temptation – one that goes back to the ancient interplay of Platonic and Aristotelian approaches to the world – to invent an abstract world that they find more attractive, for reasons that are largely methodological, than the real one. Those who take up intellectual residence in such an invented abstract world precipitate multiple failures: in the business community, among students looking to enter that community, and by encouraging the moral failure of the community itself.

Our intent is to show how the methodologies introduced into business school education combined with managerialism to foster today's world out of balance. To expose this, our book explores two themes. First, how the balance was disturbed by the obsessive preoccupation with numbers that followed the development of the "new paradigm" in business school curricula after World War Two (Locke, 1989). For people in that immediate postwar generation, numbers implied objectivity and accuracy. They were led to think, erroneously, that decisions based on numbers would be independent of the observer or of mere opinion. They also thought management could decide rationally and aspire to omniscience. But for most practicing managers not all the variables that affect their decisions and outcomes can be modeled mathematically. At the point where outcomes cannot be modeled, where numbers no longer suffice and the managers' rationality is evidently bounded, there human agency or judgment enters in to counterbalance the messages the numbers convey.

The Enlightenment philosopher John Locke called the point where people could not rely on a numbers-driven logical conclusion the moment of subjective judgment; others speak of the use of imagination, meaning that point in the analysis and evaluation where the agent's mind, for lack of a determining relationship between cause and effect, intervenes to supply her/his "subjective" solution. Those obsessed with the primacy of numbers find it difficult to accept the proposition that nonquantifiable variables have to be considered. How many times have we heard repeated Lord Kelvin's quip "if you cannot measure it, you cannot improve it"? René Descartes so disliked nonquantifiable variables that he excluded them as illusionary, as did the postwar business school curriculum reformers in the Ford Foundation program (Khurana, 2007, 233–88). Winston S. Churchill, who fully appreciated the importance numbers have for policy makers, differed; he grasped the deep significance of "soft" variables when managing events in the sphere of human action and interaction. Which is why he, as one of the twentieth century's great rhetoricians, devoted around forty minutes of thought, preparation and rehearsal to every minute of his speeches, and why those speeches were so memorable and world shaping. Men of great historical importance from Pericles to Abraham Lincoln to Charles de Gaulle have always appreciated the power of rhetoric to reach beyond "numbers alone" to bring forth and shape the agency of others. Rhetoric, as a practice of analyzing and inducing social action, goes back at least to Isocrates (436–338 BC) who felt that the distinctive aspect of Man is that he can "both persuade and be persuaded." Since in this book we argue that much of management is about numbers failing, we also argue it is more about persuasion and the shaping of others' agency than business education currently admits – and is correspondingly less about the numbers that are so clearly considered determining by so many influential business educators.

The point is that human agency counterbalances the seeming objectivity of numbers or rather comes into play where numbers leave off or fail. Quantification is generally important but seldom all-important, and sometimes it is not important at all. This also means that agents/managers must understand the limits to their agency, know where and when the numbers are determining, as well as when they are not. The French general staff, for instance, made this miscalculation in 1914. They imbibed Colonel Grandmaison's doctrine that the general who loses the battle is "the one whose will cracks first." Engaging the German army's superior firepower made this doctrine disastrous; their guns mowed French troops down – even while generals who refused to consider stopping the carnage for fear of being seen to "crack" urged them on. The irony is that the real value of training in the use of numbers springs not from denying the relevance of management's judgment, but from those managers who, being responsible anyway, fully appreciate the limitations of numbers. Those who do not know them and use numbers blindly make huge mistakes – as we might have learned from linking wartime strategic decisions to "body counts."

Unlike mathematical modeling, which rests on ostensibly universal principles, the agency analytical synthesis is always specific to a unique situation, never generalized or stored as manager-independent heuristics or Standard Operating Procedures. Agency is also profoundly morally burdened since it is not just an idea. It leads on to actions that affect others and the world. Many business entrepreneurs understood this in the past because a different culture prevailed. Business literature of the nineteenth century, even after the advent of the "robber barons," often refers to the businessman's "social duty" and the need to seek a moral balance between social and private benefit. But today, along with fetishing quantification in the business school curricula, students are trained to forget "soft" issues in the most self-destructive ideological switch that could be imagined: a switch to an ideology that has little to do with politics or religion but bears directly on how we think about management. Real business, as opposed to the models imagined and propagated by, say, University of Chicago economists, is about everything except what can be measured. Ultimately the value of measuring and modeling lies in how it helps the entrepreneurial manager focus her/his imagination on what remains: the area of uncertainty or "knowledge absence" into which entrepreneurial agency must be projected.

All significant, efficacious educational reform ultimately has significant effects on national leadership. All great reformers want their nation's elite schools to awaken a sense of national responsibility in their students. Napoleon radically reformed the École Polytechnique to enable it to train a knowledgeable and responsible elite to run his army and empire. In 1946, Charles de Gaulle set up the École Nationale d'Administration (ENA) because he believed the leadership cadres had signally failed the nation under the Third Republic. West Point, founded in 1802 and modeled on France's École Polytechnique, cultivated a culture of military and civil service; it was also the incubator of the engineer-managers who carried through many of the great civil engineering projects that served the US national interest so well during the nineteenth century.

Many people understood, moreover, that a culture of service could not be cultivated successfully in a West Point, or an École Polytechnique, or a business school merely through lectures on ethics and morality or by mindless repetition of slogans like "honor, service, and country." Knowledge about leadership is wrought at the operational business coalface or the platoon level in the military. Officer training begins with the development of interaction and trust between officer aspirants and fellow soldiers. The goal is to develop the realization that even if you do not like these guys, they are the people without whose complete confidence and unconditional full support you will certainly fail and may die. People learning this in the everyday life of the unit also learn something fundamental about themselves and their limitations. They realize that people who know nothing of their limitations do not know anything useful. The experience of being a member of something beyond the self, a certain result of being together under fire, creates a special relationship with those who shared the experience that has no match in any other sphere of life. Business leadership requires similar self-knowledge, though its circumstances are very different. Tough projects, undertaken against considerable odds and under high pressure, lead people to surprise themselves about who they are, what they can do, and how much they depend on others with complementary attitudes and capabilities.

Fully committed interpersonal association cannot be learned by an isolated student in an elite institution; it is always realized in an operational collaborative context – sociological, political, technological, geographical, historical, and so on. The military theorist Carl von Clausewitz believed military education could and should deliver this kind of knowledge, and it was implemented well in the integrated training regimes of the German officer corps between the world wars (Lewis, 1985). In contrast, the American army's policy of slotting individuals into vacant skill positions as if they were replacement parts had negative effects on unit cohesion and combat effectiveness. In this book the process of workplace association is discussed in depth because of its contribution to good management in German and Japanese manufacturing organizational cultures. In contrast, US managerialism and business school education interrupted the natural processes of association and collaboration under pressure, thereby contributing to the poorer performance of American business after the 1970s.

In earlier years US business school educators engaged the moral dimensions of managing in their technological and social educational programs. But post-World War Two reforms in the structure and content of business schools refocused student attention more narrowly and almost exclusively on the numbers, in fact, effectively banishing both soft variables and ethics from the professors' purview. Just as significant – and there is irony here – was the determination of Hayek and his generation of neoliberal economists to fight fascism by denying the theoretical possibility of fully rational centralized government. By appealing to market forces and individualism instead, these economists set themselves adrift from the very concept of community. In doing so, they pushed the "market ideology" that invaded business schools just at the time when the gap between rich and poor in the US began to increase at an accelerating pace. They brushed aside the idea that government and business leadership had complementary rather than competitive roles to play in a society in which markets function successfully.

This was a moment of profound failure of academic leadership, for the objective market forces to which these neoliberal economists appealed were not of this world. No one leading a school of general medicine will stop students from learning the practice of surgery simply because cutting the human body cannot be reduced to rigorous theory. Practical education calls for a fruitful balance of theoretical instruction and carefully guided practical experience, just as German engineering studies successfully developed and implemented *Technik* – the blending of scientific theory with workshop knowhow that is the traditional German definition of useful engineering. That US business schools failed – in part through greed, in part through the genuine difficulty of it – to develop a satisfactory way to balance abstract theorizing with a practical sense of community service and engagement is a sign of this leadership collapse. The

US business schools have generally ignored the many years of experimentation in practical and professional education – in Germany, the UK, and elsewhere – even as the latter offer good evidence of the benefits of educational balance for the former to study and, perhaps, emulate. We live with the consequences.

At the same time managerialism has led to further leadership failures. As so often in a democracy, people get what they ask for. Business recruiters have been content to let Yale, Harvard, Stanford, and the other business schools select students for them, reducing the business schools' role to one of facilitating the ambitious student's self-selection and caste membership preparation, while diminishing and maybe abandoning their educational role. In particular, business schools have been able to get away with not doing precisely what West Point and the École Polytechnique were expected to do – cultivate a culture of professional and public service. Rather, they have become penetrated by business leaders' greed, which trickles down as the students' evident sense of entitlement, limitless hubris, and general disregard for social norms that might stand in the way of their personal success. The business schools' renunciation of their moral and political responsibilities to society as they train those entering the management caste, and that caste's disinclination to have the business schools assume those responsibilities, have contributed directly to sending our lives out of balance in these difficult times.

Managerialism and business school education, 1920–1970

Management is an integral part of the post-Enlightenment democratic capitalism that spins around individualism and inter-individual relations, particularly those relations fundamental to economic activity. In the eighteenth-century Enlightenment, people began to see human progress and economic activity as related – perhaps ideally identical if we could ever get the dimensions and metrics right and see the world's uncertainty as the source of, or rather the source of the *possibility* of, human-induced growth. Growth and innovation can never be "determined" for that implies a closed system. Rather, growth is a consequence of our human ability to pull something from the realm of the unknown into the present.

Some possibilities are not present in Nature but are aspects of "things" we create, which reminds us of Giambattista Vico's notion that the "social sciences" may not be sciences at all in the sense we mean when we say "natural science" (Vico, 2000). Nature makes the things natural science theorizes. Human beings make the things social sciences theorize. The unknown from which socio-economic "things" – especially economic growth – are pulled is not one that Nature has created but the locus of human imagination, energy and action. While one can imagine all growth being the result of a specific individual's activity, a James Watt or a Henry Ford, society as we know it is "man-made," the consequence of collaboration that produces what we see as growth, the result of harnessing others' capabilities to managers' purposes. Collaboration is a hallmark of human activity, so "managing" it is a fundamental human capability without which we would have no society. Management today presupposes the agentic capacity and energy of free people. This has always been at the core of democratic capitalism, the source of its still, at times, astonishing vitality – right up to the present in places like Silicon Valley (Locke and Schöne, 2004, 16–50).

Managerialism differs; it is a phenomenon associated with membership in a specific group of managers that share specific attributes – a caste. It does not reflect the culture of democratic capitalism with its commitment to collaboration; rather the caste desires to stand apart from society, to become less social and more predatory; to see both markets and businesses as opportunities to plunder, whatever the consequences; to take unforgiving advantage of the errors, misfortunes, and circumstances of others, no matter how they arose. Managerialism has done America great harm. No aspect of that harm is more pernicious than the role business schools have played in reinforcing the caste's sense of itself and the legitimacy of its predatory instincts done in the name of good management.

Managerialism first appeared during the transformation of American organizational culture in the late nineteenth century, partially from changes in workshop routine. Explaining this change, one observer noted that around 1900:

The skill and knowledge of Europeans ... was the equal and sometimes the superior of that of Americans. The difference was in how this technical knowledge and skill was used. The European manufacturer used it to make a product. The American manufacturer used it to make a process for making a product. A high-class machinist in Europe [made] the product his company produced, his American counterpart ... set up a semiautomatic machine for less skilled labor to operate and to make this product, or he ... engaged in making the semiautomatic machine ... to make a product. The literature of the time frequently mentioned that American machines and tools were superior to the European. This, however, reflect(ed) not a difference in abilities as much as a difference in the thinking of European and American management. One appreciated the importance of and understood how to obtain the advantage from machinery, the other did not. (Litterer, 1961, 467)

To seize the advantage a new class of shopfloor managers came into existence between the worker and the owner in enterprise; these shopfloor managers developed a cluster of general factory management skills eventually codified as "scientific management," which appeared in the US soon after the turn of the twentieth century. Frederick Winslow Taylor, the most prominent person in the movement, described many of the techniques in important papers on *Shop Management* (1903) and *The Principles of Scientific Management* (1911). These techniques included time-and-motion studies that managers conducted to teach workers job efficiency, which meant among other things that managers not workers controlled skill acquisition and deployment. Taylor and other members of the scientific management community also developed a myriad of management accounting techniques (standard costing, marginal costing, budgeting, etc.) that firms implemented in the new costing departments established by managers in the pursuit of efficiency.

A second transformation led to new administrative structures, necessary to run the burgeoning corporations then changing the industrial and business landscape of the USA (Chandler and Redlich, 1961; John, 1997). Chandler and Redlich have observed the administrative problems associated with huge multifunctional firms that had fomented a managerial revolution in their administration by the early 1900s. With thousands of administrators and tens of thousands of employees, these firms threatened to become ungovernable as top managers became more and more distanced from workers and everyday operations. The resultant change separated managers involved in strategic decision-making from managers preoccupied with daily operations. Chandler and Redlich wrote

> The centralized coordination, evaluation, and planning for the diverse activities of a large number of sub-units which often carried out several different functions of production, distribution, and transportation within a single, purely private enterprise, was something new in economic history. Such needs brought the managerial enterprise into being. The new enterprise could not run efficiently without formal internal organizations. They required the generation of internal operating, financial and cost data. Only through a flow of internal impersonal statistics could control of these large enterprises be maintained. (Chandler and Redlich, 1961, 5)

In these new multidivisional (or M-form) corporations, the higher- and lower-level staffs, organized on functional bases, utilized standard cost and budgetary methods to run an increasingly complicated enterprise. The American managerial revolution, then, consisted of two interrelated aspects: it created (1) the organizational structure of the modern corporation and (2) the managerial instruments the organization used.

The resultant division of labor between top corporate management and sub-units also changed management goals.

Engineers on the shop floors and in the manufacturing divisions of M-form corporations made artifacts. Top management,
in which controllers trained in accounting increasingly replaced
the engineers, thought about money, that is, about constantly
improving return-on-investment. Money is particularly susceptible to management thinking based on general principles. As
John Quiggin remarked,

> The belief [is] that organizations have more similarities than
> differences, and thus the performance of all organizations can be
> optimized by the application of generic management skills and
> theory. To a practitioner of managerialism, there is little differ-
> ence in the skills required to run a college, an advertising agency
> or an oil rig. (Quiggin, 2003, 1)

The controller (today the Chief Financial Officer) became
the board of director's indispensable man. He was generally a
vice president in the company, with direct access to the chief
executive. His function made him a fount of information for
policy decisions of a financial, technical, and/or commercial
nature. He also had an instrumental role in policy implementation once decisions were taken. American corporations began
to create controllers in large numbers in the 1920s. The position
became significant enough by 1929 for controllers to organize
their own professional institute. These developments and their
consequences soon drew public attention. In 1932 Adolf Berle
and Gardiner Means, in *The Modern Corporation and Private
Property*, described the role of management as a functional caste
in executive circles; Simone Weil about the same time (1933)
recognized that the separation of ownership from control had
created a new "oppressive" class, as opposed to the older idea,
derived from Marx, of the bourgeoisie as an "exploitive" class
(Grey, 1996, 597); James Burnham's *The Managerial Revolution*
appeared in 1937. By World War Two the management caste

constituted, to use Heinz Hartmann's words, "a fourth production factor ... a strategic variable for the development of the firm" (Hartmann, 1963, 113). It has remained the management mindset in firms ever since.

J. David Edwards summarized the US mystique of managerialism:

1. The primary value is economic efficiency, or the pursuit of maximum output with minimum inputs.
2. Second is faith in the tools and techniques of management science and the ability of managers to use those techniques to resolve problems. In the extreme this faith in managers' specialized skills and knowledge may get carried over from the organizations they run to society as a whole.
3. Third, class consciousness, which serves as a unifying force among managers and which is perpetuated through a common literature and training regimen. This common consciousness places responsibility for organizational well-being squarely on the shoulders of managers and justifies to some degree the reliance on hierarchy and control inherent in bureaucratic structures.
4. Managerialism views the manager as a moral agent working to achieve the greatest good not only for their organizations, but for society as a whole. (Edwards, 1998, 5)

Business school education

While managerialism had taken root in American consciousness by 1940, no parallel change had occurred in management education. People often expect educational innovations to flow from two somewhat incompatible sources – academia and management practice. Between 1880 and 1941, however, neither sanctioned the creation of a science of management in business schools to accompany the new managerialism. In Great Britain, institutions of higher education ignored engineering and management education during the First Industrial Revolution (1750–1850), and almost ignored it in the Second (1870–1940). Since people in praxis and in academia rejected the idea that professors could teach management, no business schools appeared in the UK until the mid 1960s.

In Germany the story was somewhat different. While practicing managers expressed little faith in management as an academic subject, academics set up institutes of commerce (*Handelshochschulen*), and university faculties of business economics throughout the empire. They developed a science of business economics (*BWL, Betriebswirtschaftslehre*) before World War Two (Locke, 1984; 2008). The professors did not, however, pretend to research and teach management. They distinguished between a *Lehre für Führung*, a preparation for managing composed of various subjects that could be useful to practicing managers (accounting, finance, etc.), and a *Lehre von Führung*, the study of management itself. While the *BWL* professors developed a *Lehre für Führung*, they rejected the idea of management as a generic function suitable for academic study.

Even though they opted to make *BWL* a *Lehre für Führung*, the professors turned their backs on praxis. At first they struggled with the issue of whether business economics was a *Kunstlehre* (vocational subject) or a *Wissenschaft* (science); by the 1930s, however, they had opted for *Wissenschaft*, no doubt primarily in order for *BWL* to be accepted in universities (whose ethos was *Wissenschaft*). Practicing German managers thought that neither *Lehre für* nor *von Führung* in academia could train people for the job. Both sides compromised uneasily. Drawing a distinction between education that made people capable of doing a job (*berufsfähig*) and training that made them ready to do a job (*berufsfertig*), the professors decided to focus on giving students a schooling of the mind (*Denkschulung*) that enhanced their ability (*Fähigkeit*) to become *berufsfertig*. They left the training to firms and nonacademic institutions (Locke, 2008).

Between 1880 and 1940 the US business schools took up the challenge of management teaching per se as a *Lehre von Führung*, something that could be theorized with the methods of the natural sciences. This move resulted in a rapid growth in business education and in the establishment of business schools during the period. By 1950, 617 US institutions of higher education offered courses in business, mostly at the undergraduate level, with 370,000 students, nearly double the number in engineering, and 72,187 business baccalaureates graduating (Locke, 1996, 28). Although business education could not be equated with management education in all these institutions, the best US business school educators embraced the idea that they were educating a management caste or profession (Khurana, 2007).

From a curriculum perspective this claim was a fiction. American business schools did not promote progressive curricula innovation during their initial half-century. In fact the US business school syllabus of the mid twentieth century was not materially different from that of commerce schools in 1850 or even earlier, which suggests that business school growth occurred for nonacademic reasons. Various explanations have been offered. As the colleges switched strategies from their early-nineteenth-century focus on ecclesiastical matters to more secular ones, they embraced business studies, arguing loudly that it would establish management as a science. But the reasons for doing this were more likely to have been (a) to engage and serve the local business community, and thereby attract students and donations, and (b) to steal away the significant paying business education that was already being done by the many nationwide nonacademic schools of commerce.

For a long time nobody had much of an idea about what business schools should research or teach – neither the businessmen who gave money and lent their names to the new establishments, nor the professors appointed to teach in them. The subject lacked academic antecedents, so business schools up to the mid twentieth century taught traditional university subjects (geography, history, foreign languages, chemistry, physics, economics, etc.), that is, general knowledge that had little in particular to do with management, plus a cluster of commercial techniques taken from business practice – bookkeeping, merchandizing, sales, and business correspondence. This was the case even at the more established business schools. At Wharton, Steven Sass noted,

> Pioneer business professors ... found most of their curricular material in the business world, not in the universities. Despite their energy and enthusiasm, their "scholarship" essentially had been an extended form of business journalism. The heavy reliance on business for teaching material offended academic sensibilities. (Sass, 1982, 268)

Sass observed of the neoclassical-oriented economists at Wharton: "As a group the schools' economists [of the interwar period] had been cool to the practical descriptive thrust of Wharton's business programs and had had little interest in the managerial arts and sciences that were taught in those parts of the school" (Sass, 1982, 268).

In 1908, at Harvard's newly founded Graduate School of Business Administration, Dean Edwin Gay introduced the case method he was familiar with from Germany – with support from the Harvard Law School, where Langdell had adopted it some years before (Kimball, 2009). Business students read and discussed résumés of hundreds of actual cases designed to give them a taste for real business problems. The method was historical and critical rather than scientific. Indeed, the scientific method cannot be taught particularly well with cases, nor are cases very useful to researchers. The Harvard Business School (HBS), the most prestigious and influential of the US schools, did not foster the teaching of management as a positivist science.

The disequilibrium between the state of management-caste consciousness and the state of business school curricula was an incongruity. Nor would it right itself through some feedback system that looped from the early business schools into executive suites and back to the curriculum. The changes that brought about the creation of management science in business schools after World War Two came from outside. They stemmed from the cataclysmic historical events – the Great Depression, World War Two, and the Cold War – that overtook everyone. Government, stepping to the fore at these times, was more the agent of change than either business schools or businessmen. The government also helped bring many immigrants to the US, and their impact was huge. An example is the Manhattan Project, which brought people from scientific communities all over Europe to work on the US government's atomic bomb.

These events similarly disrupted the lives of the generation involved in management knowledge-creation and its transfer into business schools. An equivalent gathering of talent led to the development of a new science of management. The Cowles Commission, founded in 1932 by the Chicago businessman Alfred Cowles, which effected important contributions to mathematical economics, consisted to a large extent of immigrants. Jacob Marshak and Tjalling Koopmans, who directed the commission, were respectively Russian and Dutch. Abraham Wald, the gifted statistician who had a strong influence on the commission's work, was Rumanian by birth and partly by education (he was also educated in Vienna). Other contributors to management science also came from abroad. Trygve Maavelmo, who studied in Oslo and worked in New York during World War Two, was Norwegian. Both Oskar Morgenstern and John von Neumann, who devised game theory (published in 1944 by Princeton University Press), were Austrians. Von Neumann also contributed to the development of computers and worked with the Cowles Commission on mathematical statistics.

But the most important change agent was war itself. The team of British scientists and engineers that worked on the 'operational use of radar information' at the British Air Ministry (at Bawdsey Manor) could hardly have guessed that their efforts to solve their operational problems would have such consequences. Their success spawned operation research groups throughout the military on both sides of the Atlantic. C. H. Waddington, who was involved in anti-submarine operations along with two Nobel Prize winners and four other fellows of the Royal Society, wrote: "Never before has science been used by responsible executive authorities for such a thorough and such an unrestricted analysis of practical affairs as it was by the Royal Air Force from 1941 onward" (cited in Locke, 1989, 25).

The reference is to science, not to scientists, for it was not just a question of intelligent men and women helping out, but rather of their deploying science's methods to solve unprecedented strategic planning, logistics, and operational problems that could not be dealt with by the methods governments and military bureaucrats had hitherto employed. Operational Research (OR) projects drew on statistical and mathematically informed techniques, such as queuing and transportation theories, that were particularly suited to maximizing efficiency in large-scale military operations (Fortun and Schweben, 1993). OR's success impressed a whole generation. It impressed Winston Churchill, in particular, who noted the "clear cut, logical, mass production style of thought" that he encountered in Americans.

After a brief respite the use of science in government-affiliated agencies expanded considerably during the Cold War (Waring, 1995; Hughes, 2002; Little, 2002). In 1946, the US Army Air Corps funded a new think tank, the Rand Corporation, to help solve operations problems. In 1947, George B. Dantzig and his Rand associates developed the simplex linear programming algorithms for decision making. The procedure utilized modern mathematics (vector algebra, matrix theory, symbolic logic) and statistical techniques in an effort to take the guesswork out of decision making. The US Air Force, for instance, used it logistically in the Berlin Airlift and during the Korean War.

British and American OR and educational traditions

The question of interest here is how this OR mathematical-modeling toolkit affected business school education. Although British Operational Research during World War Two set the example for the Americans, and British OR teams were especially active in the new nationalized industries postwar, English educational tradition hobbled the development of OR studies in higher education because of a missing utilitarianism. The first university-based course, inspired by Sir Charles Goodeve of the Operational Research Club and Professor Egon Pearson, the eminent statistician, came only in 1949, and then in typical English academic fashion as a one-time, three-month evening course, not as a regular university program. A British university did not offer another short-term OR course for five years. Nor could business schools have perked up an interest in OR studies in Britain for the simple reason that, until the late 1960s, Britain had no business schools with MBA and PhD research programs, where such a transformation could have occurred.

On the other hand, US academic institutions, always interested in utilitarian education, got involved. The Case Institute of Technology in Cleveland started the first operations research (OR) unit at the urging of industry (with financial support from the Chesapeake and Ohio Railroad Co.) and the US Air Force (which funded research on airplane design). The institute organized a national conference in November 1951 on OR in business and industry attended by 150 people from all over the country (Page, 1952). Several other leading American universities established OR programs (Carnegie, University of California, Los Angeles (UCLA), Ohio State, Chicago, Johns Hopkins, Cornell, University of Pennsylvania, etc.). Among these, Ohio State and Case engaged actively in industrial consultancy from the mid 1950s on. These universities also worked with private consulting firms, some of which were large. Booz, Allen, and Hamilton, for instance, had fifty-two offices, which counseled clients on OR. Arthur D. Little got into OR early on. Generally, if private industry and consultants evinced any interest in OR, the Department of Defense readily provided funds to push the new techniques (Bonder, 2002).

Not surprisingly, since mathematics and scientific method prevailed in them, departments of industrial administration, especially in engineering institutions, pioneered the work. The OR teams at Case and the Massachusetts Institute of Technology (MIT) were good examples. Another was the Graduate School of Industrial Administration (GSIA) established at the Carnegie Institute of Technology in 1949. GSIA promoted the new paradigm and "had an impact out of all proportion to its seniority" (Locke 1989, 160). It required entering students to demonstrate a mathematical prerequisite in calculus and it employed "the analytic, normative, mathematical, and scientific mode of instruction" (Jeuck, 1973, 287). Researchers in these places, thinking the methods could and should be applied in marketing, finance, and other business disciplines, expanded beyond industrial administration. The new name given at MIT to the

Sloan School of Industrial Administration (The Sloan School of Business Administration) indicates the broadening interest. Thus mathematicians, engineers, and natural scientists, though based in technological venues, were the first to apply this new scientific method to management problems. The mathematically challenged denizens of business school faculties, generally acknowledged throughout the 1950s to be intellectually mediocre, could not have done this work.

Nor, despite their denigration of business schools, could the economists and their students in universities have pulled it off. Decades after Léon Walras turned neoclassical economics into a "mathematical science," Erich Schneider, a great admirer of his achievement, had to admit that it had not been of much help to practical problem-solving by economic policy makers (Vogt, 1979). In 1944 John von Neumann and Oskar Morgenstern had already drawn the same conclusion. In the foreword to *Theory of Games and Economic Behavior*, they wrote: "The concepts of economics are fuzzy but even in those parts of economics where the descriptive problem has been handled more satisfactorily, mathematical tools have seldom been used appropriately. Mathematical economics has not achieved very much" (von Neumann and Morgenstern, 1944, Introduction).

Game theory drew a straight line from modern mathematics (because von Neumann used algebra, matrix theory, and probability theory in his calculations) to George Dantzig's linear programming algorithms of 1947. Postwar military planners and the economists who worked with them at Rand believed the new toolkit would transform neoclassical economics into a prescriptive science. At Rand in 1948, the economist Kenneth Arrow used the toolkit in his work on Rational Choice Theory. His book *Social Choice and Individual Value* (1951) was the "first real classic" on what "is now taken as a given in economics and has spread out into many neighboring disciplines" (Bellah, 2000, 7).

The neoclassical economists Joseph Dorfman, Paul Samuelson, and Robert Solow applied linear programming to their subject as well (in *Linear Programming and Economic Analysis* [1958]). In 1954, Kenneth Arrow and Gerard Debreu announced that they had achieved a mathematical solution of general equilibrium, "the theoretical core of neo-classical economics," which Edward Fullbrook states "has become the central showpiece of academic economics ever since" (Fullbrook, 2003, 5; Arrow and Debreu, 1954).

These were heady days for Pentagon innovators. A new management technique, PPBS (Planning, Programming, and Budgeting System), was installed first in the Department of Defense by Rand economists after Robert McNamara left the Ford Motor Company to head the DOD in 1961 (Rosenzweig, 2010). After 1965 PPBS was extended to other government agencies (Locke, 1989, 33). In their enthusiasm to enhance the prescriptive value of economics, these economists set about upgrading their students' methodological skills. The Rand Corporation funded a generous fellowship program for graduate students in economics at the Universities of California, Harvard, Stanford, Yale, Chicago, Columbia, and Princeton, and provided postdoctoral grants to young faculty anxious to use the new methodology in their research (Fullbrook, 2006). Russell Ackoff left Case Western Institute of Technology to create the OR program at Wharton. Economists took their upgraded mathematical-scientific knowhow into the business schools, and the transformation of US business school education began.

Most commentators trace the radical content change in business school curricula to the impact of two reports on business education published in 1959 and the resulting efforts the Ford Foundation made to promote management education reform (Gordon and Howell, 1959; Pierson and Finberg, 1959; Khurana,

2007), even as it was clear this built on a trend begun many years before (Bottom, 2009). An explosive growth of graduate business schools and MBAs began. In 1960, some 4,814 of these qualifications were granted, 23,400 in 1970, 49,000 in 1980, 70,000 in 1990, with more than 200,000 plus per year at the century's end. The Ford Foundation programs provided funds for upgrading graduate business school faculties, in order to get rid of "unimaginative, non-theoretical teaching from descriptive practice-oriented texts to classes of second-rate vocationally-minded students" (Locke, 1989, 161).

These were also glory days for neoclassical economists. The Rand Corporation's scholarships and postdoctoral funding helped raise mathematical competence and added to the prestige of the discipline within the social sciences. That prestige grew even more when the Bank of Sweden created a Nobel Prize in economics in 1969. Most of the resulting Nobels were handed out to the creators of this new scientific-mathematical paradigm (Arrow, Samuelson, Solow, etc.). They, their students, and disciples took over teaching and research in most American university economics departments and in the best business schools, from which their influence spread overseas through the Department of Defense into NATO, through government programs such as the Marshall Plan, and through private agencies like the Ford Foundation.

In 2003 Fullbrook wrote of these neoclassical economists:

> They control the three most prestigious economics journals in which papers by their staff and PhDs predominate. Of the over 800 economists employed by the World Bank, a majority have been trained at one of the Big Eight (California-Berkeley, Harvard, Stanford, Yale, Chicago, Columbia, Princeton, and MIT). The International Monetary Fund is similarly provided, as are the other highly ranked economics departments in the US and in some cases in other countries. The 2003 edition of

Penguin's *Dictionary of Economics* ... has entries for 29 living economists. Of these, 26 ... are from the US or have had all of the most important part of their careers there. Of the 26, 100 percent have either taught at or received their PhD from one of the Big Eight. (Fullbrook 2003, 6)

What a remarkable climb to academic heights! What triumph! Yet one must be careful to clarify what this triumph means. Democratic capitalism in America turns on individualism. This is a heroic vision, part of US folklore – sustained with Horatio Alger-like stories about John D. Rockefeller, Andrew Carnegie, J. P. Morgan, and Bill Gates. When these hero-managers make "strategic" decisions in an uncertain world, they rely on intuition as much as on knowledge, for, as Maurice Merleau-Ponty says,

> Every historical undertaking has something of an adventure about it, as it is never guaranteed by any *absolutely* rational structure of things. It always involves a utilization of chance; one must always be cunning with things (and with people), since we must bring forth an order not inherent in them. (quoted in Sartre, 1948, 163–64)

From this perspective the Harvard case method makes more pedagogical sense than OR and the science of management introduced in the new paradigm; this is because the former lets students vicariously experience the difficulties of strategic decision-making in a world of bounded rationality. Professors in top business schools, who have spent so much effort since World War Two equipping themselves with the research tools of the new paradigm, see no science in historical cases and frown on them. In committing themselves to omniscient rationality, however, the neoclassical economists and other hard management science advocates produce a science divorced from reality.

After World War Two the new paradigm thrived both in the business school curricula and in the rising managerialism to be found among management practitioners, especially in the larger corporations. To the first postwar generation managerialism was not mean-spirited. It promised to provide stockholders with greater profits but also to keep the average man free from want through "managed" productivity. The rhetoric was the American response to the phony promises of Communism.

But it was rhetoric, nonetheless; managerialism in this regard was more akin to militarism than to entrepreneurship or management proper. Over sixty years ago Alfred Vagts juxtaposed the terms "militarism" and "the military way." The military way meant setting a military goal and developing the most efficient organizational means to see to its accomplishment. It required unpredictable and at times unfathomable genius. Management, as applied to commercial and industrial organization, meant the same. "Militarism," on the other hand, had a much different connotation. As Vagts wrote:

> [It] presents a vast array of customs, interests, prestige, actions and thought associated with armies and wars and yet transcending true military purposes. Indeed, militarism is so constituted that it may hamper and defeat the purposes of the military way. Its influence is unlimited in scope. It may permeate all society and become dominant over all industry and arts ... Militarism displays the qualities of caste and cult, authority, and belief. (Vagts, 1937, 11)

Managerialism as opposed to management means "a vast array of customs, interests, prestige, actions, and thought" associated with but nonetheless transcending the need for the efficient running of commercial and industrial organizations. In this book we argue its influence and power in enterprises is now almost unlimited in scope, having expanded into almost every kind of organization in the USA, profit and nonprofit, commercial and educational, governmental and military. As it grew up

in America in the second half of the twentieth century, managerialism came to exhibit the features of a caste – cult, authority,
and belief – that Vagts noted. American managerialism – given
the mystique it generates in elite business schools and the ethos
being taught there, so evident in the media's championing of the
wisdom, capability, and invincibility of our CEOs, and in the
laws and customs that empower them – developed into a system
that has, most paradoxically, often denied organizations the very
means needed to formulate and effectively reach their goals.

Few, other than leftist ideologues, would have expressed
such dark thoughts before 1970. Now, after the economic
crisis of 2008, these views are commonplace. How can this
be? The postwar generation that developed managerialism
and business school education presided over an unprecedented US-led expansion of wealth and power. Its participants attributed that growth to their own knowledge and
skills, eschewing any sense of propriety or respect for the
others who also made contributions. Now some chickens are
coming home to roost – but whose are they? How are we to
understand that American plenty began to disappear after
1980, evident in the growing gap between rich and poor, and
in the US's diminished global power? Do America's managers
carry responsibility for this too?

Our argument is that they do – in part – and just how much is
our central topic. There can be no proof, of course, for there is no
real nonmanagerialist model against which we might compare
what happened. The way of historians is to gather various items
of evidence and deploy them as rhetorical support for conclusions that seek to be no more than reasonable and illuminating
of our current situation. To justify our conclusions, we begin
by arguing that the vision and optimism that propelled managerialism were not systemically based but historical, arising in a
window of time and space. That is, rather than being based in a

powerful science of managing or even on a securer grasp of an enterprise's problems and challenges, managerialism was little more than a fad, a tale we told ourselves, but one that became leveraged into America's culture. From that position managerialism had a huge impact on enterprises in the US and elsewhere, and on nations themselves and how they began to be managed. We argue business schools contributed significantly to this impact. As corporate managers in the 1980s began to place their own interests above those of the nation or of the other stakeholders, they found such questionable personal inclinations supported by the culture-wide adoption of the language of free markets and antiwelfarism.

In Chapter 1 we look at how this cultural shift accelerated, even as one aspect of Edwards's definition of managerialism waned quite early on: "faith in the tools and technique of management science and the ability of managers to use those techniques to resolve problems." We help explain what went wrong with what Edwards called "the primary value of managerialism – its economic efficiency." The gathering evidence of managerialism's ineffectiveness as an approach to everyday practice, as manifest in the formal modeling of managerial decisions and organizational processes, was no impediment to its spread, as "Groupthink took hold" (Janis, 1972).

In Chapter 2 we explore how managerialism failed to develop an ethical core or commitment, what Edwards called the second component of managerialism, presenting "managers as ... moral agents working to achieve the greatest good not only for their organization, but for society as a whole." In Chapter 3, moving from the macro to the micro level, we discuss the failure of managerialism to meet the organizational challenges of the US automobile industry. Chapter 4 describes how the management caste's conscious preoccupation with money (and the ideology of greed) disrupted the financial system and brought it to the edge of ruin in the early twenty-first century. Clearly the trust initially placed in managerialism, and in the transformative power of business school education, too frequently resulted in inefficiency and impotence.

The Conclusion focuses on prescription – on guidelines for restoring the life presently out of balance. Given the extent of the current crisis of governance, many commentators presume society must change. There is a clear divide between improvement and correction, and radical change. Those looking for remedies within managerialism and the business school establishment forget Albert Einstein's admonition that one cannot solve problems at the same level of thinking that created them.

CHAPTER 1

The failure of management science and the US business school model

In this first chapter, as throughout the book, we are not concerned with establishing the truth value of management as "science" in our critiques of managerialism and the new paradigm in US business school education. That discussion we leave to management theoreticians and philosophers of science. Nor are we particularly concerned with the interpretations of historians, politicians, journalists, and social scientists, with various axes to grind, of recent US management events. Instead, we let the historian's old rule of thumb serve as a guide in our presentation, namely that informed contemporaries who witness events and often participate in them, usually, unless misinformed about or unaware of facts, get the story right the first time around as they live it. Since contemporaries close to events deftly wield Occam's razor, they best tell the story about the failures of management science and the US business school model, failures which, particularly in the past forty-plus years, surprised and puzzled most Americans in and outside of management, and still do those who are unwilling to suspend disbelief.

The first event of contemporary assessment covered in this chapter is the usefulness of war-spawned operational research techniques in the solving of complex postwar management problems. The chapter then turns to an assessment of a different order. It discusses the inability of Americans equipped with the toolkit of the new paradigm to cope with the greatest challenge US manufacturing faced in the second half of the twentieth century, that coming from Japan. This story is not told in ruined companies and unemployed people (Locke, 1996, 158-75) but in a critique of the epistemology of the new paradigm in management disciplines introduced postwar in the business schools. The seismic shift in consciousness that the epistemological arguments entailed infiltrated discussions about Japanese manufacturing culture. The debates affected the thoughts and lives of many people. The life of one prominent business school professor, H. Thomas Johnson, is used as a reference point to illustrate the change and the resistance to change that occurred, as managerialism and the business schools struggled to preserve their newly established orthodoxy.

The chapter's last section looks at business schools' relations with praxis after 1980 when, with the scientific standing of the faculties improved, top business schools had turned into research institutions, with multiplying subdisciplines and proliferating peer-reviewed scientific periodicals. The concluding section weighs contemporary views about how well graduates educated in the reformed business schools performed in the two major events that shaped the US economy in the mid-1980s – the Japanese manufacturing challenge and the industrial revolution in information technology (IT).

The OR experience: the new paradigm in postwar business schools

There were critics right from the beginning of what Locke called "the New Paradigm" (Locke, 1989, Chapter 2) and Schlossman, Sedlak and Wechsler (1987) the "New Look" in business school education. Among them were members of the old descriptive school in economics and business studies who distrusted the mathematicians. Fearful that their models poorly mirrored reality, sure, in any event, that mathematics would make business studies incomprehensible to businessmen, and hence separate them even more from academia, they often put up a spirited resistance (Larsfeld, 1959; Marschal, 1940; Koch, 1960; Mattessich, 1960; Piettre, 1961; Howson, 1978; Hudson, 2010). But it was difficult to defend the point of view of the old pre-mathematics paradigm, since the victory of the new men would make non-mathematically schooled business economists' views seem academically passé, and their protests self-serving. Besides, the powerful technical arguments of the self-confident purveyors of mathematical omniscience had to have their day. Until more numerate as well as nonnumerate people had experience with the new techniques, a telling body of criticism could not appear. When they did, the doubters began to assemble.

It is easy, therefore, to find maverick critics cavorting outside the citadel of a new discipline while the victory bells are still ringing inside. Doubts, however, crept up within the ranks of operations research scientists themselves. Since the OR experience in the two pioneering OR countries (Britain and America), as noted in the Introduction, somewhat differed because of academic traditions, OR appraisals varied somewhat within OR societies in each country.

There was more of a conflict in Britain between academia and working OR people and, because of the lateness and sluggishness of OR's academicization, a greater imbalance between the two. It was as if the academic version of OR did not take root in the UK as it did in the United States. That version was dominated by abstract, complex, highly theoretical mathematical models which, because of academic career conventions – publish or perish – captured the scientific OR journals; the American academic version was carried into British OR academia belatedly through contact with Americans. K. B. Haley notes that Russell Ackoff's arrival at the University of Birmingham, as Joseph Lucas Visiting Professor, in 1961 was the signal event. "His presence had a major impact on the whole of the UK educational scene, inspired a number of initiatives in the way the subject was viewed in industry, and was one of the prime movers in the establishment of the Institute for Operational Research" (Haley, 2002, 85). The University of Birmingham, which had invited Ackoff, had instituted a master's in OR in 1958; his presence there seemed to stimulate the development of academic OR in the UK, with master's degrees in OR initiated at Imperial College London and at Cranfield in 1961; while a master's course in the subject started at the University of Hull in 1962.

The British *Journal of the Operational Research Society* (*JORS*) began, under the influence of US OR, to reflect the greater formal scientific attributes of US OR, for, increasingly, the scientific articles in it came from academics employed in American educational institutions. Patrick Rivett's analysis of the articles published during one twelve-month period observed that "of 103 papers, 81 were by academics of whom only 31 were British. The *Journal* had over half of the papers in the form of theoretical materials from overseas academics" (Rivett, 1981, 1057). Considering the large size of British OR society membership (Table 1.1), the vast majority of working OR people, that is, the vast majority since the academic operational research group was so small in the UK, did not publish. Rivett claimed that "80% of OR people go through life without publishing anything" (Rivett, 1981, 1057).

Perhaps UK executives could themselves better appreciate nonacademic compared to academic OR people because of UK businessmen's disregard of academic qualifications. Board-level executives in the top 100 UK corporations had significantly lower levels of education compared to, say, their French counterparts, even after the big push to upgrade levels of education for UK businessmen in the late twentieth century. Whereas in 1998 in France, 44.5 percent of board members of the 100 largest corporations had diplomas from the top ten ranked schools and 90.5 percent of them at the graduate degree level, only 16.4 percent of board members in the largest 100 UK corporation had diplomas from the top ten schools, and of them only 38.1 percent were graduate degrees (McClean, Harvey, and Press, 2007, 542).

There was hardly any complaint in the *JORS* about the absence of OR studies in British universities. On the contrary, articles primarily criticized the OR that was taught in them. Practical OR people even denied the relevance of the mathematical models proffered by academics, arguing that they were a poor yardstick with which to judge the health of OR in Britain. N. R Tobin, K. Ripley, and W. Teather, in "The Changing Role of OR," observed:

> In the Third International Research Conference on OR and Management Science at Bowness in April 1979, more than one attendee was left with an impression of a widening gap between the university-based OR man and the in-house OR man, the former full of gloom and despondency because OR is not being used in any important areas, the latter ... often carrying out useful OR in quite important areas. (Tobin, Ripley, and Teather, 1980, 279)

The implication is that a dichotomy existed in British OR between the academics following the Americans and the practical men who still gave useful advice to British management because they ignored the abstraction of the academics. Apparently, large numbers of OR scientists in Britain, like businessmen, shared the traditional and deep-seated English suspicion of academics. Both the OR Society and its journal, like all British professional associations, were started by practitioners, not academics. "The low proportion of academic members in the [Operational Research Society] reflects the growth of the UK Society as a body to encourage the exchange of practical experiences" (Haley, 2002, 85).

Practical OR people in the UK and the US believed that their work benefited clients, and there were successes in this regard. The petroleum industry's decisions on product mixes were never the same after the publication in 1952 of "Blending Aviation Gasolines: A Study in Programming Interdependent Activities in an Integrated Oil Company" (Cooper, 2002; Bixby, 2002). Given that in this case a demonstratively better decision process provided an optimum solution to a financially important decision problem in a competitive market, the better decision procedure, mathematical programming, was widely adopted for an entire class of tractable problems. If such particular successes could have been generalized, the expectation would have been that, with more experience in dealing with problems and perfecting their methods, the proportion of successes to failures would significantly increase through time. Actually, the opposite happened.

In 1981, Dando and Bennett evaluated the evolution of the mood of UK operational researchers as reflected in the pages of the *Journal of the Operational Research Society* (*JORS*), by looking at the issues published in 1963, 1968, 1973, and 1978. The credo affixed to the masthead of the journal when it started had read:

> Operational Research is the application of the methods of science to complex problems arising in the direction and management of large systems of men, machines, materials and money, in industry, business and defence. The distinctive approach is to develop a scientific model of the system, incorporating measurements of the factors such as choice and risk, with which to predict and compare the outcomes of alternative decision strategies or controls. The purpose is to help management determine its policy and actions scientifically.

Up to 1968 when "optimism about the future of OR" reigned, there was "almost a total lack of criticism and debate in the journal." In 1973, papers began to enounce considerable doubt about the practical effectiveness of OR, a doubt which by 1978 was being voiced in about one quarter of the major papers appearing in the journal. The essays of the late 1970s were, therefore, a culmination of a decade of ever-increasing and deepening concern about the usefulness of OR at the very center of the new paradigm.

The pessimism deepened when the subject of long-term prediction came up. The comments of Roger Collcutt on planning studies for a third London airport illustrate this concern. He observed that "alternative sites [for the airport] cannot be reliably distinguished by OR or any other method other than political. [About all that OR studies could do] was suggest the feasibility of various futures which in certain circumstances may look desirable" (Collcutt, 1981, 368). With all the "mays" and "mights," a defense of OR obviously conceded much to its critics.

A stagnation if not decline in Operational Research Society memberships also indicates that all was not well. Whereas membership grew between 1964 and 1974 at an annual rate of 20 percent, subsequently growth rates fell dramatically (Rivett, 1974). Table 1.1 furnishes comparative data on OR professional society participation in France, Germany, the United Kingdom, and the United States. OR groups in these four countries were, in terms of numbers of qualified members, the four largest in the world. Among these four groups, two, the British and American, were by far the largest, judged both in terms of members per million inhabitants, and members in absolute numbers. Of the two leading countries, the British were slightly ahead of the Americans in membership per million inhabitants. These two nations dominated the operations research movement; indeed, whereas in 1980 OR societies in the UK and the US had 13,371 members together, those in all of Europe had only 4,720. The doubts that had cropped up had occurred in the countries where OR had the greatest experience and following.

Table 1.1

Membership in operations research societies in Europe and the USA

Country	Year OR society founded	Qualified members 1974/76	Members per million population 1974/1976	Qualified members 1980	Members per million population 1980
France	1956	570	11	555	10
Germany	1957/ 1961	701	11	749	12
UK	1953	2,808	51	3,371	60
US	1952	11,000	51	10,000	47

Source: H.-J. Zimmerman, "Trends and New Approaches in European Operational Research." *Journal of the Operational Research Society* 33 (1982), 597–603, 598.

Since operations research and management science are generic terms, misgivings about their efficacy actually covered a variety of managerial activities. They pertained to OR work in firms and in local and regional governments. Wilbert A. Steger pointed out that during the 1960s "a virtual avalanche of urban/regional models about new planning, program analysis, budgeting and other 'futuristic' decision-making and policy related decision-making [appeared]" (Steger, 1979, 548). But he noted how unsuccessful the OR techniques were: "When reviewing this era, it is difficult not to wonder at the relative lack of sophistication ... [T]he assessment techniques ... proved not to be very useful and often caused more damage than good in dozens of overly literal applications." In the US, criticisms extended to the management techniques adopted in the national bureaucracy, the most famous being the Planning, Programming, and Budgeting System (PPBS) installed in the Pentagon in 1962 and in 1965 extended to other government agencies. Although designed to make decisions scientifically, that is, to optimize the means by which tasks are decided and realized, PPBS, Waddington observed, "has failed everywhere and at all times. Nowhere has [it] been established and influenced governmental decisions according to its own principles. The program structures did not make sense to anyone. They are not, in fact, used to make decisions of any importance" (Hofstede, 1978, 460). In 1972 the PPBS system was terminated (Gruening, 1998, 8).

No group so fundamentally misread reality as those who implemented and used PPBS in the Pentagon during the Vietnam War. The complaint, moreover, is more than political. It is also technical, for PPBS did not fail just because the Americans who implemented it were discredited by the Vietnam venture. They lost the war because they also did not understand the limitations of rational management methods such as PPBS, limitations prescient people knew at the time (Rosenzweig, 2010).

Other government scientific management techniques produced similar outcomes – in President Carter's attempt to implement a sibling of PPBS, the Zero Based Budgeting

Procedure in the federal administration (abandoned because of its "inadequacies"), in the introduction in French administration after 1963 of a scientific management process similar to PPBS (RCB, *Rationalisation des Choix Budgétaires*), which suffered, people later discovered, from "excessive hope" (Lequéret, 1982, 16). The reasons for meager results of optimization techniques in governmental affairs and operations are complicated. An important one is that the complexity of the decision problems in real government organizations makes optimization impossible; the irreducible characteristics of the problems grossly violate the assumptions required by the various optimization techniques. Another reason – one which is not always acknowledged – is that governmental problems amenable to optimization sometimes have great difficulty attracting the political attention and funding required to optimize.

"OR problems can never be a perfect representation of a problem," the OR guru Russell Ackoff concluded, in a startling volte-face at the end of the 1970s (Ackoff, 1979, 102). "They leave out the human dimension, the motivational one;" indeed, he affirmed that the successful treatment of managerial problems deserves "the application not only of science with a capital S but, also, all the arts and humanities we can command." Arts and humanities take mythopoetic dimensions of decision problems into consideration that express tacit-bonding skills and even sensory modes of communication essential to collaborative work.

For people managing nationally important operational events, imaginative management thinking should have started where the numbers left off. With managers captive to numbers-determinant thinking, too often excessive violence, environmental destruction, social disruption, waste of public resources, and national disgrace resulted.

Crumbling epistemologies:
a critique of the new paradigm

While contemporaries questioned OR, at a more profound level they also in the 1980s scrutinized the epistemological foundations of management sciences – indeed of traditional science itself – in a powerful dissent from the postwar consensus about managerialism and the value of the toolkit that neoclassical economists had introduced into business school education between 1960 and 1980. The debate had a practical dimension because it encompassed the organizational challenge that Japanese manufacturing now posed to American managerialism, and it had serious consequences because as people changed their minds, this disrupted careers.

The transformed life of one management expert, H. Thomas Johnson, illustrates the practical consequences of this intellectual revolution. In the 1980s Johnson was a professor of management accounting at a respectable university (Johnson, 1978); a decade later, at a less prestigious but nevertheless respectable institution, he had become a Professor of Quality Management. This change – no quick jump onto some faddist bandwagon – amounted to a considerable pilgrimage during which Johnson came to question the value and usefulness of what he had been doing – at great personal cost because the business school where he worked in the early 1980s denied him tenure for challenging the new paradigm his academic peers had assumed he would use to frame his courses on management accounting. Johnson's focus on historical field research was denounced by his academic accounting colleagues who were trained to see the world exclusively through the lens of finance, efficient markets, and agency theory.

Along the way, Johnson spent several years studying the Toyota Production System, took a seminar with W. Edwards

Deming, and investigated new developments in physics. In a letter (Locke, 1996, 176) he mentioned three books in particular that influenced his outlook during his metamorphosis: Peter M. Senge's *The Fifth Discipline: the Art and Practice of the Learning Organization* (1990), Robert W. Hall's *The Soul of Enterprise* (1993), and Fritjof Capra's *The Turning Point: Science, Society, and the Rising Culture* (1982). Two of the three books are about management, but the other, Capra's, is not a management book at all; it deals with the reevaluation of the foundations of science.

On the assumption that much can be learned about a person's (or a generation's) behavior from reading the books he/she absorbed, the books Johnson cited can be used to shed light on his transformation and that of like-minded contemporaries. The following reconstruction of Johnson's intellectual migration is not, it must be cautioned, necessarily about the specific intellectual and psychological steps in the transformation Professor Johnson underwent. He never explained precisely how and when the books affected his thinking; he only wrote that they did. However, if the books do not catalogue the exact process of transformation of anyone, including Johnson, they do offer one representative insight into the thought process of Everyman who changed his/her view about American managerialism during the 1980s. Taken together, the three books permit the reader to construct a fantasy about the epistemological collapse of American managerialism.

The story begins with Capra's *The Turning Point*. Here, he planted an intellectual and psychological seedbed in which dissent from American managerialism could thrive and grow. Capra's analysis permitted people to map a very important intellectual revolution onto a significant historical event – the industrial challenge of Japan to America (for self-confident Americans, a troubling thing). The University of California physicist asserted that a systemic crisis in Western science not only questioned its intellectual foundations but raised doubts about the ability of traditional science to solve pressing human problems.

Capra begins with a statement about how people in "think tanks" and "brain trusts," expressing "mainstream academic views," have been unable by their own admission "to solve the nation's most urgent policy problems." Capra traces this impotence to what Alfred North Whitehead called "the century of genius," the seventeenth, when Isaac Newton worked out the mathematical basis of physics, René Descartes its dualist philosophy, and Francis Bacon the experimental method that subsequently led science from triumph to triumph. Descartes proclaimed that "all science is certain, evident knowledge; we reject all knowledge which is merely probable and judge that only those things should be believed which are perfectly known and about which there can be no doubt" (Capra, 1982, 47).

The experimental method that brought "certain" results in physics is called reductionism. Reductionism assumes that matter is "the basis of all existence" and that the material world is composed of "a multitude of separate objects assembled into a huge machine." Consequently, complex phenomena can best be "understood by reducing them to their basic building blocks and by looking for the mechanisms through which these interact." Although physics led the way, the reductionist methodology eventually permeated all the sciences.

Capra contends that the Western view of scientific method has crashed and that the first discipline to crash has been physics itself, where the Cartesian philosophical foundation and the reductionist methodology had seemed most secure. Capra's chain of doubt begins with Heisenberg's statement that "every word or concept, clear as it may seem to be, has only a limited range of applicability," a statement that plays havoc with Descartes's "certainty" principle. Capra claims that two discoveries of modern physics fundamentally discredited the Newtonian world. First, quantum theory proclaimed not only that subatomic particles – electrons, protons, neutrons – are not the solid objects of classical physics, but that they are very abstract entities which have a dual aspect.

> Depending on how we look at them, they appear sometimes as particles, sometimes as waves, and this dual nature is also exhibited by light, which can take the form of electromagnetic waves or of particles ... The more we emphasize one aspect in our descriptions, the more the other aspect becomes uncertain, and the precise relationship between the two is given by the uncertainty principle. (Capra, 1982, 47)

The second discovery Capra noted pertains to the nonlocal connections of individual events. We can never predict the jump of an electron from one atomic orbit to another; we can instead only predict its probability because the behavior of the electron is affected by the nonlocal and unknowable connection to the whole. Nonlocality stops us from being able to determine cause and effect precisely – we have to fall back on statistical probabilities. The concepts of nonlocality and statistical causality, Capra affirms, "imply quite clearly that the structure of matter is not mechanical ... [but that] the universe [is] more a great thought than a great machine" (86).

The new physics Capra describes abolished Descartes's separation of mind from matter. The result, Capra observed, is manifest in scientific investigation itself.

> Human consciousness (in quantum physics) plays a crucial role in the process of observation ... My conscious decision about how to observe, say, an electron will determine the electron's properties to some extent. If I ask a particle question it will give me a particle answer. The electron does not have objective properties independent of my mind. (87)

This discovery overthrew Newtonian epistemology; it meant that the patterns scientists find in nature connect intimately with the patterns of their minds, with their "concepts, thoughts, and values." Consequently, the universe is perceived as a dynamic "web of interrelated events." Since none of the properties of any part of the web is independent, reductionism is devalued. Since all the parts follow the properties of the other parts, "the overall consistency of their interrelations determines the structure of the entire web" (93).

In subsequent chapters Capra observes that all of modern science realizes that "scientific theories are approximations to the true nature of reality, and that each theory is limited to a certain range of phenomena." Moreover, researchers have questioned the reductionist method over and over again in other sciences. Biology, which Capra discusses in detail, where life, under the reductionist theory, "had to be understood in terms of cells," now increasingly studies "the organism as a whole. [B]iological functions [are] seen as the result of the interaction between the cellular building blocks" (103). The contention, then, is that the really interesting questions are about how the cells interconnect, how the cells must be understood in terms of a whole organism, not the individual cell itself. If the cell alone is examined, the observer might come up with a view of cell processes that fails to fit those of the whole organism. Capra extends the same antireductionist theme to the psychological and social sciences, of which he singles out behaviorism and economics for special criticism.

Throughout, Capra adopts a systems view of knowledge, wherein systems are defined as "integrated wholes whose properties cannot be reduced to those of small units" (21). Within systems "the behavior of the individual part can be so unique and irregular that it bears no sign of relevance to the order of the whole system" (238). For our purpose Capra's choice of an organic metaphor to illustrate the social aspect of systems theory is heuristically valuable:

> Bees and ants are unable to survive in isolation, but in great numbers they are almost like the cells of a complex organism with a collective intelligence and capabilities for adaptation far superior to those of its individual members. This phenomenon of animals joining up to form larger organismic systems is not limited to insects but can also be observed in several other species, including, of course, the human. (277)

Capra's systems approach undermines nineteenth-century social Darwinist ideas about individual competition. The individual is not only imbedded within a system but is directly involved in that system's self-organization. The tendency of living systems to form multilevel structures, "whose levels differ in their complexity is all-pervasive in nature and has to be seen as a basic principle of self-organization" (280).

The application of systems ideas to human organizations makes them fundamentally different in their patterns from the consecutive "stacking of building blocks," or the hierarchy of command–power relations so familiar to the Newtonian outlook and to Chandler's view of the modern US corporation. Borrowing Arthur Koestler's concept of the "holon," something that is simultaneously a whole and a part, Capra points out that "every subsystem is a relatively autonomous organism while being a component of a larger organism." And he extends the idea of dual identity – of a relatively "autonomous organism ... being a component of a larger organism" – to the mind. "In the systems concept of mind, mentation is characteristic not only of individual organisms but also of social systems. As Bateson emphasized, mind is immanent in the body and also in the pathways and messages outside the body. There are larger manifestations of mind of which our individual minds are only subsystems" (280).

This statement has radical implications for an understanding of group mental activity and the individual's place in it. It also alters our view of social order. Capra's comments on this subject deserve to be quoted *in extenso* because they describe a fundamental shift in views about organizational behavior:

> The multileveled structure of living organisms, like any other biological structure, is a visible manifestation of the underlying processes of self-organization. At each level there is a dynamic balance between self-assertive and integrative tendencies, and all holons act as interfaces and relay stations between systems levels. Systems theorists sometimes call this pattern of organization hierarchical, but that word may be rather misleading for the stratified order observed in nature. The word "hierarchy" referred originally to the government of the Church. Like all human hierarchies, this ruling body was organized into a number of ranks according to levels of power, each rank being subordinate to one at the level above it. In the past the stratified order of nature has often been misinterpreted to justify authoritarian social and political structures ... To avoid confusion we may reserve the term "hierarchy" for those fairly rigid systems of administration and control in which orders are transmitted from the top down ... By contrast, most living systems exhibit multileveled patterns of organization characterized by many intricate and nonlinear pathways along which signals of information and transaction propagate between all levels, ascending as well as descending. That is why I have transformed [hierarchy] into a tree, a more appropriate symbol for the ecological nature of stratification in living systems. As a real tree takes its nourishment through both its roots and its leaves, so the power in a systems tree flows in both directions, with neither end dominating the other and all levels interacting in interdependent harmony to support the functioning of the whole. (Capra, 1982, 281–82)

These were the ideas Professor Johnson encountered in one of the three seminal books he read. The management books by Hall and Senge that also influenced Johnson's "migration" incorporate the transformed outlook that Capra identified: from the Newtonian, mechanistic, reductionist view of science to an organic, systemic view. Robert Hall in *The Soul of Enterprise* (1993) called for a new, holistic form of manufacturing in which companies do not preach teamwork between customer, employees, and suppliers, while management makes decisions. He presents a scheme which contrasts the old hierarchical spirit with the new, in which all elements in a thriving system are integral to the entire system's well-being and are interconnected. The systems metaphor for Hall's new management dynamic is not the machine, the power hierarchy of classical American management, but Capra's tree, with the roots and leaves, all parts, sustaining the life of the system (Hall, 1993, 84).

Peter Senge's book, in which the author combines systems theory with processes of continuous improvement, concurs:

> Systems thinking leads to experiencing more and more of the interconnectedness of life and to seeing wholes rather than parts. Whenever there are problems, in a family or in an organization, a master of systems thinking automatically sees them as arising from underlying structures rather than from individual mistakes or ill will. (Senge, 1990, 375)

Senge recognizes different goals in the learning process. He writes about them in terms of personal mastery (connectedness), systems thinking (interconnectedness), shared visions (commonality of purpose), and team learning (alignment). He writes too about the differences being increasingly subtle.

Just as Capra notes of the physicist, "ask a particle question, you get a particle answer," Senge notes of the manager, if you ask a systems question you get a systems answer. And the opposite is implied – ask a managerialist question you get a managerialist answer. The phrases and reasonings Senge uses echo Capra's views – the metaphor of the tree, the values and thought patterns of the observer coloring reality, the web of interconnectedness of the single unit with the whole, the extracorporeal extension of the mind to group "thinking." The connections between both Hall's and Senge's system modes of perception and Capra's are obvious just as they are multiple.

So are the connections between Capra's work and the Japanese productions systems that people, including Johnson, began to study intensively in the 1980s. Capra does not mention Japanese management, but people found certain beliefs dwelt upon in his book central to it. Moreover, if Capra did not write specifically about Japanese management, those who did, if without reference to him, often did so in Capra's terms. In some cases the terms are identical. The Research Team for Japanese Systems, sponsored by the Masuda Foundation, spoke of Japanese management as "An Alternative Civilization," using Arthur Koestler's "holon" concept to clarify its position: "The Japanese organization is constructed from a system base of sub-whole and sub-individuum, and it may be most appropriate to view the Japanese organization as a holon made up of contextuals" (Masuda Research Project Team for Japanese Systems, 1985, 15).

Three well-known contemporary works (Fruin, 1992; Kenney and Florida, 1993; Nonaka and Takeuchi, 1995) and two from Johnson (Johnson, 1992; Johnson and Bröms, 2000) made similar connections. Johnson's work will be discussed in Chapter 3, but the others can be used here to show how Capra-like concepts can be found in the literature about Japan. Kenney and Florida wrote in *Beyond Mass Production* (1993, 8) that the "underlying conceptual premise of the book is that Japan is at the cusp of a new model of production organization that mobilizes workers' intelligence as well as physical skill." They stress how the Japanese enterprise uses teams and other organizational techniques that explicitly harness workers' knowledge at the point of production, thereby transforming the ordinary employee's knowledge and intelligence into a source of value. They insist on the integrative, organic nature of the Japanese work process. They are, as in the following passage, not talking about hierarchy or Taylorism, but about reciprocal action, interconnection:

> We refer to this organization as the new shop floor [where] innovation becomes more continuous and the factory itself becomes a laboratory-like setting. The underlying organizational feature is the self-managing work team that enhances the functional integration of tasks. The new shop floor thus integrates formerly distinct types of work – for example R&D and factory production, thus making the production process very social. In doing so the organizational forms of the new shop floor mobilize ... the collective intelligence of workers as a source of continuous improvement in products and processes, of increased productivity, and of value creation. (Kenny and Florida, 1993, 6)

Correspondingly, Mark Fruin writes of the Japanese corporation building:

> A stair-step process of give-and-take, of interaction, and integration between various production functions, and the welding of this interactive, feedback process into a product-development system ... Variability results in learning and learning is the basis of a strategy based on functional integration, innovation, and continual improvement in manufacturing ... Factories as architectures of innovation [appeared imbued with] the conviction that institutions can think, learn, and act for the purposes of self-improvement and self-renewal. (Fruin, 1992, 214)

Institutions that "think, learn, and act" – such words clearly conjure up Capra's biological references to nonlocal connections of individual events to the whole, of the universe as a great "thought," instead of a machine, of the "web of interconnected-ness" where the properties of parts map with the properties of other parts.

Nonaka and Takeuchi (1995) built their case about knowl-edge-creating companies on their ability to harness both tacit and explicit knowledge. Kenichi Yasumuro observed how sensi-tive Japanese engineers understood the necessity to learn tacitly as well as explicitly when importing Western technology at the end of the nineteenth century (Yasumuro, 1993). Nonaka and Takeuchi related that the interaction between these two knowl-edge sources, one with its locus in the skilled labor force, the other in the upper levels of management, is the dynamic of knowledge creation found typically in Japanese but rarely in Western corporations. In the West an

> intellectual tradition can be traced back to Cartesian dualism ... A is pitted against B, resulting in the 'A vs. B' model ... The debates over subjective vs. objective, mind vs. body, rationalism vs. empiricism, and scientific management vs. human relations reflect this intellectual tradition. The danger ... is to create the building blocks of organizational knowledge creation in the same light. In our view, tacit knowledge and explicit knowledge ... are not opposing ends of a dichotomy, but mutually complementary entities. They interact and interchange into each other to create something new. (Nonaka and Takeuchi, 1995, 236)

Nonaka and Takeuchi acknowledged Peter Senge's attempt to overcome "the Cartesian dualism" by integrating "reason and intuition," but they also felt that Senge himself was too much caught up in the mind/body duality characteristic of Cartesian thinking. This prevented him from appreciating the importance of "the body-learning aspect of tacit knowledge" and hence stopped him from fully appreciating the source of knowledge creation at play within the Japanese company.

Educational alternative

One further point needs to be made about Japanese organization culture and US business school education during this era. For people living in Japan, the latter was irrelevant. Most rich and powerful NGOs and businessmen that wish to call on society to fulfill a need, usually find a way to achieve their ends. This happened in the US when rich businessmen endowed business schools in famous universities to teach the managerial caste. After World War Two, Japanese employer associations repeatedly requested more and better higher education in Japan. They asked for scientists, engineers, computer specialists, for the creation of technical research facilities and for the establishment of closer cooperation between universities and industry. But the words "business school education" seldom appeared in these requests because the presence of a powerful outside class of managers schooled in general management principles in business schools made no sense in company cultures based on a "web of interconnectedness." Since business and industrial spokesmen presented no real and persistent demand for this education and there was no business school establishment in Japan to lobby for it, no American-style education of the MBA type materialized (Locke, 1996). In the 2007 *Business Week* survey of the top US and international MBA programs, 191 are located in North America, 22 are in England, 10 in France, 60 in the rest of Europe (but only 3 in Germany) and 1 in Japan.

This does not mean that the Japanese had no interest in management education outside business firms and professional organizations. But they did it in a way Americans would not recognize as management education, although it very much suited Japanese organizations. Educational specialists observe that, despite changes in education brought on after World War Two through Western emulation, the cultivation of group consciousness retained its focus in Japan. William K. Cummings noted that Japanese teachers spend an inordinate amount of time at the beginning of the school year just establishing order in the classroom, so that learning subsequently can take place. "Classroom order is developed by having students cooperate in groups that prepare contributions for the rest of the class" (Cummings, 1990, 150).

Classes break into groups, with teachers sitting by rather unobtrusively. Bright students work with slow learners whose performance they help raise to the group pace. Teachers and administrators do not discipline individuals, by, say, sending a pupil to the office, but let the group to which the problem pupil belongs decide and administer "punishment." Assertive discipline is "antithetical" to the Japanese style of student management. Japanese teachers even at the preschool level defer discipline authority to pupils. Small work groups are held collectively responsible for homework assignments, so that if a group member does not do this work, the others receive demerits. Groups are assigned tasks, sometimes too difficult to do, just to see how well they can handle them – they are stretched (Adams, 1995, 69).

Process education stresses the procedure through which results are obtained, not the results themselves. W. Edwards Deming, after working in Japan, emphasized process as opposed to individual performance. He advocated making improvements in the process in which the individual works, not trying to eliminate individual "mistakes" (Deming, 1982, 1986). Kaoru Ishikawa's famous fishbone diagrams used in Japanese schoolrooms and in manufacturing illustrate process orientation; they show the people involved how the entire process in which they work produces the results, so that they can learn to think of their work in terms of process improvement. In other words, in a high-employee-dependent Japanese management system, management education takes place differently than in America. It occurs cooperatively in the primary, intermediate, and secondary school system, not in business schools. If people wish to organize a work process in which the employees participate in managing it and are not "managed" by a group external to it, what happens in the Japanese classroom K through 12 *is* management education.

At the tertiary level, Japan's educational environment differs as well. Japanese firms want to hire educated people; since they do not intend to hire them into management slots like in big US corporations, they are much less interested in recruiting specialists in management subjects than people right out of college with arts and science degrees from elite universities. The subjects Japanese learn were and are not all that different from those studied in advanced and advancing countries all over the world – and where American education is judged to be deficient, despite the demands of the "new paradigm," namely in mainline disciplines such as mathematics, natural science, engineering, and, to a far lesser extent, social science. Serious students who want to get jobs, like students everywhere, usually avoid majoring in the humanities; they do study commerce, but not management in graduate schools (unless they are seconded by a big firm to Harvard or some other US or European business school, not to learn the techniques, but to learn about Western business culture and to make contacts). In Japanese corporations, core employees, as distinguished from temporary employees, are not recruited by skills but as people whose chief qualification must be a capacity to assimilate quickly the corporate work culture and production systems. Recruited students have no company-and-job-specific skills. Companies spend much time and money on in-house training, job rotation and multiskilling that impart tacit and explicit learning tailored to the firm's environment.

Business school response to major economic events

Since the introduction of the new paradigm into US business schools occurred *after* the onset of managerialism, it played no role in its triumph. The corporate hierarchies Chandler describes already existed in 1960. The recruitment of the first MBAs equipped with the "New Look" toolkit began in the early 1970s; their rise to positions of importance in corporate hierarchies came in the mid 1980s. The question to pose, then, is what role did the schools and graduates from the "New Look" reformed business schools play in the innovative economic events of the mid 1980s? Two problems in particular were significant: meeting the Japanese manufacturing challenge, and promoting the revolution in information technology (IT).

Business schools: not meeting the Japanese manufacturing challenge

Americans conscious in the 1980s of the new epistemology and the need to reform US manufacturing to meet the Japanese challenge cursed the "New Look" in US business school curricula. Johnson complained about it in *Relevance Regained* (1992, 175–96), and in an article he wrote with Anders Bröms in 1995 (Locke, 1996, 287), and he returned to the theme in the book he wrote with Bröms in 2000. He observed:

> Successful [US] managers believed they could make decisions without knowing the company's products, technologies, or customers. They had only to understand the intricacies of financial reporting ... [B]y the 1970s managers came primarily from the ranks of accountants and controllers, rather than from the ranks of engineers, designers, and marketers. [This new managerial class] moved frequently among companies without regard to the industry or markets they served ... A synergistic relationship developed between the management accounting taught in MBA

programs and the practices emanating from corporate controllers' offices, imparting to management accounting a life of its own
and shaping the way managers ran businesses. (Johnson and
Bröms, 2000, 57)

He despised these lifeless pyramidal structures imposed on
work processes and managed by computer-oriented production
control experts:

> At first the abstract information compiled and transmitted by
> these computer systems merely supplemented the perspectives
> of managers who were already familiar with concrete details of
> the operations they managed, no matter how complicated and
> confused those operations became. Such individuals, prevalent
> in top management ranks before 1970, had a clear sense of the
> difference between "the map" created by abstract computer
> calculations and "the territory" that people inhabited in the
> workplace. Increasingly after 1970, however, managers lacking
> in shop floor experience or in engineering training, often trained
> in graduate business schools, came to dominate American and
> European manufacturing establishments. In their hands the
> "map was the territory." In other words, they considered reality to
> be the abstract quantitative models, the management accounting
> reports, and the computer scheduling algorithms. (Johnson and
> Bröms, 2000, 23)

People studying the transfer of Japanese manufacturing to
America also objected to the US management caste's work
culture. Japanese transplant managers criticized the American
managers they encountered for their lack of "commitment" and
their abuse of power. They complained about the US managers'
caste mentality, about their weak loyalty to their companies,
about their high salary claims, and about their inability to forget
Taylorist modes of command management – all mother's milk
in managerialism and taught in the core curriculum of US business schools. Martin Kenney and Richard Florida in their study

of Japanese transplants emphasized this point: "In nearly every plant we visited [in the US], Japanese managers voiced concern about the manner by which American managers operate. An executive at Honda of America told us that his greatest problem was teaching American managers the Honda way" (Kenney and Florida, 1993, 287).

Like-minded people thought US manufacturing and the business schools that funneled MBAs to them were ripe for reform. The management problem in manufacturing came to public attention. In 1979, after the NBC television program "If Japan Can ... Why Can't We?" three to four hundred alarmed managers trooped into each of W. Edwards Deming's four-day seminars on Total Quality Management (TQM), which heretofore had been empty. Concern became a movement with institutional dimensions. The Greater Philadelphia Chamber of Commerce sponsored PACE, the Philadelphia Area Council for Excellence, which brought together businessmen, union leaders, and civic dignitaries grappling with regional deindustrialization attributed to Japanese competition. A Growth Opportunity Alliances of Greater Lawrence (GOAL), composed of the same sort of people as PACE, met for the same reason during the same period. Deming Societies sprang up in every region of the country, more than fifty of them by the late 1980s, eagerly resolved to propagate the master's ideas about statistical quality control and process management, the mainstays of Japanese production systems.

In the Rust Belt, concerned people broke away from the American Production and Inventory Control Society, with its quantification-oriented Material Resource Planning (MRP), a computer-focused control system for shop floors created at IBM in the 1960s, and founded the Association for Manufacturing Excellence (AME), headquartered in Wheeling, Illinois. Formally chartered in 1985, AME concentrated initially on manufacturing improvement. They investigated Japanese production methods, employee participation schemes on shop floors, and team-based work. AME grew into a national association with 5,000 members, organized regionally, with branches in the Northeast, the Mid-Atlantic, the Southeast, the Midwest, the West, the Southwest, and Canada.

Congress in the 1988 Trade Act authorized the US Department of Education to found sixteen (later expanded to twenty) Centers for International Business Education and Research (CIBER). Business school deans, seizing on the opportunity, organized new CIBER units in their precincts, which emphasized foreign languages and business cultures. They organized foreign business internships, and study exchange programs. Some of the new institutes blossomed, such as Hawaii's Pacific-Asian Management Institute (PAMI). Business schools offered joint MBA-Asian Studies degrees, at Cornell, the University of California at Berkeley, Michigan, and Wharton.

But these developments, which took place on the periphery of business school education, did not disturb the core "New Look" study program in elite MBA institutions. Considering the magnitude of the threat, the failure of the business schools to throw themselves into the fight to save manufacturing is astonishing and constitutes a leadership failure of major importance. Robert S. Kaplan, former dean of Carnegie Mellon Business School and a Harvard Business School professor (co-author with H. Thomas Johnson of a critical book on management accounting, *Relevance Lost*, 1987), underscored the failure. After reviewing articles published in leading operations management journals and examining research and teaching in top business schools, Kaplan found that only 1 to 2 percent of the schools had "truly been affected, as of early 1991, by the Total Quality Management revolution that had been creating radical change in many US and worldwide businesses" (Kaplan, 1991, 1). He concluded that American business school research and teaching contributed almost nothing to the most significant development in the business world over the past half century – the quality revolution.

The information technology revolution and business schools

While manufacturing declined in what became the Rust Belt, the nation experienced a remarkable industrial revolution in information technology that for most allayed doubts about the prowess of US entrepreneurship, except for those mired in the old decaying industrial regions. Could it be that business schools made up for their neglect of TQM by making a major educational contribution to the management needed to develop the new IT firms?

In order to clarify the relationship between business schools and the IT revolution, our discussion is divided into two time frames: 1950–1975, the pre-commercial phase of development, and 1975 onward, the stage of interactivity in IT technology that exploded on the internet in the 1990s in commercial applications that fundamentally changed almost every aspect of people's lives throughout the world. To have made a major contribution to the management of the IT revolution would have made the business schools' neglect of TQM forgivable.

Before 1975

"According to modern theory," Erkko Autio and Riikka-Lenna Leskela wrote, "economic growth is ultimately driven by the search for new ideas by profit-seeking innovators" (see Reynolds et al., 2001, 28). This thinking belongs to the triumphant school of neoclassical market economists. The historical economist Werner Sombart offered a better explanation for the rise of Silicon Valley before it happened. He claimed that "the growth of large-scale nationalistic warfare" was the root cause of economic development, since the demand for more effective weapons, offensive and defensive, stimulated technology and invention (quoted in Castells and Hall, 1994, 17). The industries that developed IT before 1975 operated "outside the restrictions of [commercial] market criteria." They were an accidental product of the exigencies of the Cold War. Not greed, not free-market demand, but fear, especially after the Soviet Union exploded atomic bombs and possessed the intercontinental missiles to deliver them, prompted Americans decades-long to pay the enormous costs of superpower rivalry. Most of that money went into conventional weaponry, but billions also went for scientific research in IT. Consequently, one group of scholars observed: "From the explosion of the first Soviet atomic bomb in 1949 until the mid-1960s, the driving force for science policy remained the military-technological competition with the Soviet Union" (Alic et al., 1992, 97).

Most of the interactive IT exploited commercially after 1975 started in government-sponsored research. Without a long and expensive gestation period, IT could never have been used commercially, for it would not have existed. Examples are legion, but one, because it is now ubiquitous, suffices to illustrate the noncommercial origins of IT. The government lavishly funded a new organization, the Advanced Research Projects Agency (ARPA) in a crash program to regain the initiative in science and technology (which in fact the US had never lost). In 1964 a team of ARPA funders visited Douglas Englebart, whom the National Aeronautics and Space Administration (NASA) had supported with computer equipment and one million dollars a year to establish an Augmentation Research Center at the Stanford Research Institute, to "create the mind amplifying computer" he had been writing about (Rheingold, 1991, 81).

In 1969, the Englebart research team presented their findings at a computer conference.

> Sitting on stage with a keyboard, screen, mouse, and the kind of earphone/microphone setup pilots and switchboard operators wear, Englebart navigat[ed] through information space ... He called up documents from the computer's memory and displayed them on the big screen at the front of the auditorium, collapsed the documents to a series of descriptive one-line headings, clicked a button on his mouse and expanded a heading to reveal a document, typed in a command and summoned a video image and a computer graphic to the screen. He typed in words and deleted them, cut and pasted paragraphs and documents from one place to another ... The assembled engineers, programmers, and computer scientists had never seen anything like it. (Rheingold, 1991, 84)

Englebart's ARPA-supported center introduced the interactive features of the personal computer that Apple purloined and brought to market in the 1980s and which is now omnipresent.

The networks that link computers, moreover, began as government projects, starting with SAGE (Semi-Automatic Ground Environment System), a computer-activated, real-time continental air-defense system developed at the Massachusetts Institute of Technology's Lincoln Laboratory under US Air Force contract, continuing through ARPANET, a computer network that ARPA researchers created and exploited themselves in their research liaison and then gave to the commercial world (Locke, 2000, 70). None of the technology originated with commercial application in mind but instead as tools needed to solve military information problems. The United States' massive commercial IT lead after the 1970s arose from the government-sponsored head start, not from superior free-market enterprise (Lerner, 1992). To conclude with Rheingold,

If necessity is the mother of invention, it must be added that the Defense Department is the father of technology: from the Army's first electronic digital computer in the 1940s to the Air Force research on head-mounted displays in the 1980s, the U.S. military has always been the prime contractor for the most significant innovations in computer technology. (Rheingold, 1991, 80)

The hardware industry thrived before 1975; semiconductor firms evolved from small producers of made-to-order military products to mass producers of standard chips. The industry expanded capacity, became capital intensive and vertically integrated. By 1980 only a few American semiconductor producers (Fairchild, Intel, National Semiconductors, Advanced Micro Devices) counted in an industry that employed 200,000 people in Silicon Valley alone. Management in the semiconductor industry adopted the budgeting, the accounting-based financial reporting systems, and the cost-control instruments typically found in large managerial corporations. Consequently there was a useful place for MBAs in them just as there was for business school graduates in financial accounting in US automobile firms during the era of mass production.

But then, just as in automobiles and at about the same time, the "technology jelly bean" producers suffered grievous losses through Japanese competition. Between 1983 and 1990, US firms' share of worldwide semiconductor revenues fell from 80 percent to 33 percent (Locke, 2000, 74). The industry looked as if it too would succumb to the Japanese challenge. But the explosive growth in interactivity technology and software manufacturing unexpectedly transformed the region and the American IT industry, resulting in a remarkable US high-tech manufacturing turnabout.

The US IT industry moved away from a semiconductor, commodity-driven business to one of high-value-added specialized chip making, and high-tech, customized semiconductor production. More important, IT bred a prodigious software industry in the 1980s. By the early 1990s, over 5,000 software firms operated in the United States.

Did managerialism make Silicon Valley commercially successful after 1975?

How a dynamic habitat like Silicon Valley really worked in the high-growth commercial phase of information technology is not easily deciphered. For explanations, scholars turned away from big firm hierarchies to habitat analysis, since start-up firms drove the development. No social scientist could actually build a high-tech habitat based on habitat theory and then watch it blossom commercially before his or her eyes. The life-giving variables were not sufficiently knowable to do it. But it can be said upfront that the management ideas MBAs learned in the reformed business schools did not drive habitat development in these high-tech regions.

In the start-up enterprises mushrooming in the Silicon Valley habitat after 1975, scientists and engineers, not MBAs, were the heroes. Those from Stanford's Computer Science Department illustrate the point. Andy Bechtolsheim, a founder of Sun Microsystems, John Hennessy, a founder of MIPS Technologies, Inc., Jim Clark, a founder of Silicon Graphics and Netscape, Jerry Kaplan, a founder of Techknowledge, Go, and Onsale, Forrest Basket, technical officer at MIPs, Len Bosack, a founder at Cisco Systems, and David Cheriton, a founder of Graniote Market Value all came out of there. In 2004 the combined worth of their companies amounted to about $90 billion. The scientists and engineers possessed the indispensable mathematical and scientific knowhow for the great product ideas essential to start-up firms.

Business schools object to such a formulation, on the grounds that entrepreneurialism requires more than a technical idea; to succeed, a high-tech start-up needs a sense about the commercialization of a product, plus capital, public relations, marketing, and good administration, which are not technical ideas. There is no evidence, however, that those trained in mainline MBA business schools with skills suited to management in pyramidal corporate structures spurred entrepreneurship in a high-tech cluster such as Silicon Valley. Most studies about it and similar habitats stress entrepreneurial networking. The Swedish economist Gunnar Eliasson, who was often in Silicon Valley, noted that the new Experimentally Oriented Economy there, which operated in a climate of "uncertainty," depended on the existence of "competency blocs" (Eliasson, 1998); Michael Best talked about success depending on an "open system dynamic" in a regional network into which start-up firms integrated and from which they profited (Best, 2001).

Eliasson observed that "the bulk of subjects on the teaching agenda of business schools, like investment calculation and financial economics, rest on the assumption of [a formal knowledge] model" (Eliasson, 1998, 6). And the angel investors that funded IT start-ups had to know the "territory" for their investments to do well. AnnaLee Saxenian pointed out that the informal networks of moneyed angels brought technical skills, operating experience, and a myriad of industry contacts – as well as cash – to the ventures they funded (Saxenian, 1994, 184). The closeness to local technology networks was the key. She quoted a former Wall Street executive on their importance: "In New York, the money is generally managed by professional or financial promoter types. Out here [Silicon Valley] the venture capitalists tend to be entrepreneurs who created and built a company and then sold out. When problems occur with any of their investments, they can step into the business and help." Tacit knowledge about IT learned in Silicon Valley made up more of venture capital competence than formal knowledge of financial and investment techniques learned in business school finance courses.

The people who developed Silicon Valley in the post-1975 commercial phase were a motley crew. Many of them were immigrants from Asia who had come to study mathematics, science, and/or technology in American universities and then stayed on to work in firms, start their own companies, or both. Saxenian told their story based on the 1990 census (Saxenian, 2000). At the century's end, Asian immigrant entrepreneurs had founded 17 percent of Silicon Valley high-tech start-ups. Almost simultaneously, IT centers developed in their homelands – in Taiwan, in Singapore, in Bangalore – incited through the Silicon Valley connection.

The extent to which Europeans participated is less clear (Locke and Schöne, 2004). They began to take part in what Frenchmen called the gold rush, the *ruée d'or,* in the mid 1980s. Jean-Louis Gassée, who arrived at Apple then, was one of the pioneers. The great influx came in the 1990s. Numbers are not easy to derive, but those provided by the French consulate in San Francisco estimated that from 10,000 to 40,000 Frenchmen were in Silicon Valley and San Francisco circa 2000, which, even if the lower number is used, is a lot of French scientific and engineering talent living in northern California. Most of them came from the *grandes écoles* of engineering. Rumors about German visitors put their numbers even higher – twice that of the French. They were scientifically knowledgeable and numerate, but there were few MBAs among them because MBA programs in Germany were rare. The British arrived in great numbers too, although they are less easy to identify because they blended more easily with the Americans. Every European country had a presence.

Orthodox American managers in the late 1970s expected their management views to be just as useful to firms in maturing

IT companies as in low-tech enterprises. John Sculley, the Wharton MBA, thought so when he decided to leave Pepsi-Cola for Apple in 1983. He told Steve Jobs,

> Just as Northern California is the "technology center" for innovation in computers ... the Northeast corridor [is] the "management center" for innovation in business. There are a lot of exciting concepts and tools being developed by business schools and consulting firms in the East ... Make sure you are exposed to their leaders and their ideas. (Sculley, 1987, 135)

The top-down style of management, with its top-down management control methods, that he had known at Pepsi-Cola and learned at Wharton and naïvely thought would be the East's contribution to management at Apple did not work. These methods were useless for habitat networking. They did not even succeed at Apple. Sculley found this out after his management team ousted Jobs. A new, Sculley-led board managed the firm rapidly towards bankruptcy. Desperate stockholders forced the board to bring back Jobs, a product man, to save the firm; Sculley was history, Jobs the future.

The burgeoning software industry depended on a tacit-knowledge work environment that could not easily accommodate MBA managerialism. Tacit skill and innate ability are more pertinent components of the software programmer's competence than they are that of engineers working on hardware. The largest software firm (Microsoft) hired "people with no professional programming experience or formal training." Neither of its two founders (Paul Allen and Bill Gates) had obtained college degrees. The legend of Silicon Valley hacker/entrepreneurs is not a myth; they learned about programming on the job, when they had a gift for it. Software firms, in their maturity, moreover, never assumed the organizational dimension of large manufactories. Even Microsoft employed only 700 people in its new facilities at Redmond, Washington. In the late 1980s the core workers there, the programmers, required "a work environment," as Ichbiah and Knepper remarked, "with as few restraints as possible. At Microsoft, the company chooses the best, hardest-working people and turns them loose to prove themselves" (Ichbiah and Knepper, 1992, 225).

Much the same conditions prevailed within the specialist chipmakers, whose business by the late 1980s outpaced that of the commodity-driven, mass-production microchip makers. The specialist chipmakers discarded the control mechanism learned in business schools for network organizations "where people teams, and sometimes whole organizations," as AnnaLee Saxenian wrote, "act as independent nodes, form multiple links across boundaries, support one another, share common values, and report to a matrix of leaders who act as coaches and mentors more than line managers" (Saxenian, 1994, 90).

Business schools under the influence of the new paradigm did not teach this kind of management. People learned it from the entrepreneurial environment. Once the schools awoke to the nature of the IT habitat's entrepreneurial demands, they began belatedly to develop centers of entrepreneurship out of sheer opportunism. Professors and students in the add-on business school centers participated in the activities of habitat entrepreneurial start-up networking. But the faculties in the top research business schools resisted, in the name of management science, efforts to make entrepreneurship an academic discipline. Indeed, Stanford's business school faculty is notorious for having refused to accept the endowment of a chair in entrepreneurship from a rich benefactor because they considered the subject scientifically unworthy. There were no Nobel prizes in economics to be won in the subject.

By 2000 the "New Look" that had been ushered into business school education had clearly prepared people inadequately to meet the Japanese challenge or fully participate in the entrepreneurial opportunities of Silicon Valley. Students in economics departments and business schools started to revolt against their neoclassically trained economics professors. In June 2000, a group in Paris openly protested about the "knowledge censorship" they experienced in their studies. They proclaimed in a public manifesto:

> Most of us have chosen to study economics so as to acquire a deep understanding of the economic phenomena with which the citizens of today are confronted. But the teaching that is offered, that is to say for the most part neoclassical theory or approaches derived from it, does not generally answer this expectation. Indeed, even when the theory legitimately detaches itself from contingencies in the first instance, it rarely carries out the necessary return to the facts. The empirical side (historical facts, functioning of institutions, and study of the behavior and strategies of the agents ...) is almost nonexistent. Furthermore, this gap in the teaching, this disregard for concrete realities, poses an enormous problem for those who would like to render themselves useful to economic and social actors. (Fullbrook, 2003, 6)

The French rebels called the neoclassical economics they were learning "autistic," meaning that it was cut off from the real world. They named their movement, Post-Autistic Economics (PAE). The manifesto of protest, published in *Le Monde*, gained the attention of the French government, which promised "investigations." The rebellion initiated a broad if thin and unevenly spread international movement that involved mainly professional economists, who founded their own review (originally called the *Post-Autistic Economics Review*, now the *Real-World Economics Review*), currently with almost 12,000 subscribers. But these doubts about the effectiveness of the "New Look" in business school education grew mostly outside the United States, on the fringes of core MBA programs within business

schools, and in less famous institutions. The professorial establishment in prestigious US economics departments and business schools skillfully deflected the attack by the most effective
way of doing such things – ignoring it. They insisted on living
in an academic cocoon, doing research that produced theories
without real-world substance, publishing it in peer-reviewed
journals, to be read by academic audiences, while training their
best graduate students to follow in their footsteps by making
careers depend on mastering the toolkit and lingo of the new
paradigm.

CHAPTER 2

US managerialism and business schools fail to find their moral compass

Emissaries of US managerialism and business schools invariably believed, even if they were conservatives, in the liberal credo, as Benedetto Croce phrased it, "that the aim of life is in life itself and duty lies in the increase and elevation of this life and the method in free initiative and individual inventiveness" (Croce, 1963, 20). They exported this credo as a new moral as well as material order. But after a good beginning in the free world living under Pax Americana, the twentieth century ended with people generally questioning the ability of US managerialism and business school education to build a moral order based on such a credo. This moral outcome has somewhat surprised Americans, who for decades have been used to thinking of their system as a positive moral force in the global community.

This chapter's discussion of the failure to find a moral compass deals first with the management caste (managerialism) and then turns to business school education. Managerialism during the third quarter of the twentieth century, in the heyday of mass production capitalism, earned kudos for creating the mighty productive engine that made Americans a people of plenty. Only, about 1980 a serious demoralization set in. Moral judgments about post–World War Two business school education also changed during the last two decades of the century, after the new paradigm had revolutionized business school teaching and research – and the bloom had gone off the rose of triumphant postwar US managerial capitalism.

The chapter also examines great religious establishments outside America (those treated are Islam, Confucianism, and Christianity in Germany) that came to provide a moral compass in management matters that US managerialism did not, and, therewith to offer alternatives to the current moral bankruptcy of American managerialism and business school education. US Christianity is also discussed, in this context, for not providing the missing moral compass that thoughtful Americans now generally agree they need for social order. Nor did the academic establishments in the United States – the last subject the chapter takes up – which are charged ostensibly with educating the elite. Without the moral dimension in their education, the life of the governing class spun out of balance.

Managerialism's missing moral compass

In order to handle moral dimensions, historians have to adopt a method of investigation that does not distort the record. The massive and rapid industrialization of Europe and the United States in the nineteenth century led, because of the popularity of Marxist socio-economic theory, to a great deal of confusing discussion about how values systems diverged in various countries. Marxists held a convergence view that the socio-economic process gave birth concomitantly to new classes and to the belief systems that the bourgeoisie, and the management caste it created, embraced. But Val R. Lorwin, the American historian of French labor, wrote shortly after World War Two that "Citizens of a country, which has not passed through a feudal age, cannot easily imagine how long its heritage conditions social attitudes" (Lorwin, 1954, 7). From this perspective, if a society industrialized without adopting bourgeois values, clearly something went "askew." As early as 1916, Thorsten Veblen attributed political-social divergence in Germany to a persistence of feudalism. Similar observations have been made about Japan: in the course of modernization Japan imported Western economic and financial institutional models, but that importation did not drastically alter cultural values inherited from the country's feudal past (Westney, 1987).

If the citizens of a country that has not passed through a feudal age cannot imagine the effect this heritage has on subsequent industrialization, by the same token, citizens of a country that has not passed through a liberal-democratic revolution before fast-paced and intense industrialization takes place cannot imagine how that liberal-democratic heritage conditioned social relations in that industrial state. In short, nothing inherent in the process of massive industrialization in late nineteenth-century America made people more liberal or democratic or individualistic. America had a different political and economic history during the late nineteenth century from feudal Germany and Japan because America had undergone a liberal-democratic revolution *before* large-scale industrialization and the rise of management hierarchies and business schools began.

There is schizophrenia among historians about this subject because of a failure to remember that the political and social situation of a country before industrialization preconditions attitudes on questions of moral order when that society industrializes, as much as the industrialization process itself later determines outlooks. For Veblen, Joseph Schumpeter, and many others who were familiar with the American experience, the feudal hangover in Germany produced an aberration in the "normal evolution" of the industrial society. It was an atavism, something to be cursed for distorting the country's history. What happened in America politically, socially, and morally was deemed a normal evolution. A post-1945 generation of German historians (the Hans-Ulrich Wehler school) plowed this furrow, claiming that the failed revolution in mid-nineteenth-century Prussia saddled Germany with an anachronistic bureaucratic-autocratic military state that stopped the country during its rapid industrialization from developing normally like Britain and America, with terrible consequence for the German nation, namely World War One, defeat, and Hitler. Industrialization brings great social upheavals, but the economic process can accommodate and adapt to quite diverse political and social heritages, and quite successfully, too. Germany and Japan were not atavistic; they were just different.

That is one issue affecting our treatment of the subject of moral order; the other is religion. Throughout recent history, religious belief and attitudes towards moral order have been entwined. People have grown to be especially conscious of the connection during the era of globalization. Nothing better illustrates the role of religion as a moral compass for management and management education than the resurgence of Islam. It is our first religious topic, not because Islam has a great presence in the USA, although it is growing, but because it is leading a moral–religious counteroffensive against the once-triumphant credo of US managerialism and business school education, which is now morally moribund. The second religious topic is Confucianism, chosen not because China is the USA's great economic rival but because the Chinese government is promoting Confucian moral philosophy, instead of an ethic of neoliberal individualism, as a moral compass for a rapidly transforming society. Finally, religion as a moral compass is discussed with regard to Christianity because of the role that

Christians in Germany played in establishing a consensus about a moral order in company governance based on codetermination, which contrasted with American Christianity's fervent embrace of managerialism. The discussion does not pretend, therefore, to present the rich and nuanced beliefs of each religion but only, as is appropriate in an essay, to select out and sketch essential tenets that elucidate the relationship between managerialism and moral order. The chapter closes with a discussion of the moral bankruptcy of secularized US academia, with an emphasis on business school education.

Islam

One powerful voice, the Pakistani Abul Ala Mawdudi (1903–1973), appealed to the traditional idea of the universal Muslim community, the *umma*, which rests on the principle of Islamic solidarity. Undifferentiated except by gender, the *umma* is supposed to rise above trivial national, regional, and local ties. Having its own laws, values, and convictions, it should be the focus of every Muslim's loyalty and the source of his/her identity. Probably the Ayatollah Khomeini most forcefully expressed this view. Timur Kuran observes that Khomeini wished "to subordinate all objectives to the general goal of restoring the centrality of Islam in private and public life" (Kuran, 1997, 20–21).

Islam is narrow-minded. This narrow-mindedness does not apply to religious belief itself. In the Quran Allah respects the right of non-Muslim peoples to practice their religions, which they have done almost unimpeded for centuries in Muslim lands. But Islam is a religion of orthopraxy. Traditionally it insists more on correct behavior than correct doctrine (orthodoxy). A good Muslim is not someone whose beliefs conform to an accepted doctrine but whose commitment to Islam is evident through observable behavior, although there is latitude in this regard (Smith, 1958, 20). Smith explains that "the Islamic counterpart to the Christian concept of heresy is bid'a," which means "deviation," and has traditionally been interpreted to mean "behavioral non-conformism." For Muslims the regular recitation of sacred texts is considered to be important even without the exact comprehension of their meaning; even in non-Arab lands, the call to prayer and the prayers themselves are always in Arabic, a language few understand (Kuran, 1997, 9).

What matters to devout Muslims is poetry, not prose – the wedding between mystical meaning and words, not words and thought; the heart-lifting Arabic cadences of "La ilaha illa Allah," not its literal English translation, "There is no god but God." Modern Christians and, of course, management scientists often misunderstand the psychological comfort ritual induces – its mystical spiritualism. Hearing the sacred texts in Arabic, committing them to memory, following exactly the ritual of prayer, brings man into mystical union with God more effectively than the words of dialecticians. Orthopraxy makes Islam publicly visible. It lays out the terrain on which controversy takes place. Orthopraxy puts psychological pressure on Muslims everywhere. Whereas Christians have been shedding outward trappings of their faith, Muslims have been putting them on. Muslims are increasingly asserting themselves.

Westerners are somewhat puzzled. The puzzlement has much to do with different views about the content of education. Since Christians cannot believe that the Bible in its many translations is the actual word of God, memorizing it does not have the same meaning for them as memorizing the Quran has for Muslims. Through the Quran God speaks directly to the people. He speaks in Arabic; they are His words. To commit them to memory lets people, much like Christians feel it in the Eucharist, experience the living God.

Islamic economics: an oxymoron?

Premodern religious practices projected into the modern era (cutting off people's hands for theft, stoning women convicted of adultery, compelling women to cover their bodies in public places, wearing the burqa, and many others) are particularly troublesome for a religion characterized by correct public behavior (orthopraxy). The general struggle between Islam and the West and within Islam about the content of the orthopraxy is not our concern here. But we are interested in the commercial shariah and in particular in the Islamic Economics that emerged in the Muslim world as a counterforce to the moral bankruptcy of managerialism.

Most Muslims do not accept the idea that in affirming Allah, they are anti-modern. Indeed, the accusation that they are is the crux of resurging Islam's dispute with the West about morality. Otto Hahn, the German Nobel Prize winner, raised the issue in 1937 in a letter to his colleague Max Planck. After acknowledging that science is not incompatible with religion, he added, "But there are many areas where religion and natural science have nothing to do with each other. Natural science is a stranger to all ethical questions" (Berninger, 1974, 12). If we accept this view, and that economics is a science, which the "New Look" in business studies proclaims, then any attempt to introduce ethics into economics and/or its fellow management sciences (e.g. finance) is "unscientific."

Thoughtful Muslims could never accept a definition of economics that excluded morality, nor the assumptions upon which neoclassical economics is based, i.e., the economic man, maximum utility, and greed. They do not argue logically or empirically against Western economists, with subtle points about epistemology – but religiously. Muslims exalt man as a moral being, made in the image of God, subject in economic matters as in all others to the strictures of religious teaching. For centuries Islamic jurists developed a sophisticated corpus of contracts for various types of trade transactions particularly suited to commercial economies. These laws merged with others in the shariah. The term means "way" or "path"; it is the legal framework within which public and some private aspects of life, including economic aspects, are regulated for people living in a legal system based on Islamic principles of jurisprudence, as befits a religion concerned with orthopraxy.

Islamic economics operates according to the rules of shariah known as *Fiqh-al-Mu'amalat* (Islamic rules of transaction). Mostly Islamic law does not conflict with international transaction standards, but sometimes it does. In particular the Quran and the Hadith prohibit usury, the collection and payment of interest, also commonly called *riba* in Islamic discourse. In addition, Islam prohibits investing in businesses that are considered unlawful, or *haram*, for example businesses that sell alcohol, or pork, or that produce pornography, which violates Islamic concepts of dignity and virtue. And it rejects the notion that people can escape financial commitments through bankruptcy.

Law faculties in Islamic universities traditionally dealt with shariah law. But the oil boom in the 1970s brought money, and a resurgent religion the zeal, to carry though the building of an educational infrastructure for Muslims that specifically concentrates on Islamic economics and shariah law in financial education and economics. Timur Kuran notes that "new institutes of Islamic economics [are coming] into being, and departments of Islamic economics [are being] started in various parts of the Islamic world" (Kuran, 1997, 24). Not surprisingly, because of its location, one of the first, a Center for Research in Islamic Economics, was founded in 1977 at the King Abdul Aziz University, Jeddah – "To co-ordinate and support research into Islamic economics." Also not surprisingly, because of old

British imperial connections, the Islamic Foundation (UK) established an Islamic Economics Unit in the City of London even before (in 1976) the one in Jeddah (in 1977).

Since then the UK Islamic Foundation has published twenty-six "highly accomplished" books on Islamic economics, an *Encyclopedia of Islamic Economics*, in cooperation with the Centre for Islamic and Maghreb Studies (London) and the University of Loughborough, and started a *Review of Islamic Economics*. After 1991, hundreds of people – bankers, finance specialists, lawyers, accountants, researchers, and students – participated in annual seminars organized by the Islamic Economics Unit in association with the Islamic Development Board and the University of Loughborough.

In the UK, banks have gotten increasingly interested in shariah-compliant mortgages for their clients. While just one bank offered them in the mid 1980s, ten did by 2004, to the more than two million Muslims living in Britain. Other institutions offered Islamic finance in finance courses. The School of Oriental and African Studies (SOAS) in London offers such a course (Brignall, 2004, 1). Meanwhile, the institutionalization of studies in Islamic countries proceeds. The International Association for Islamic Economics, established in 1984 with the support of Muslim banks, set out to reconstruct economic and financial theory and practice in the light of Islamic principles. The association ties together a number of universities in the Gulf States.

UK institutions used distant learning to extend Islamic management education into Muslim states. Cass Business School, headquartered in the City of London – "the largest home to Islamic Finance outside the Islamic World" – created an Islamic Finance MBA through Dubai, aimed at fund managers, investment consultants and advisors, and a wide range of professionals in banking and in the financial services sector more broadly.

To these distant learning courses from Europe, circuits were added in Asia. The International Institute of Islamic Business and Finance, homebased in India, networks into the United Arab Emirates, Sri Lanka, Bahrain, Qatar, and other Muslim regions. Its courses are certified by the professional groups Islamic Banker, Islamic Insurance Professional, and Islamic Investment Analyst. It offers a Diploma in Islamic Finance and a Diploma in Management.

This list of achievements is hardly exhaustive, and their creation does not mean that the Muslim world stopped studying Western economics. On the other hand, it does mean that in a few short years much has been done to draw attention to Islamic economics as Muslims attempt to wrest control over their own destiny through education. Westerners might, from their perspective, call it nonscientific, but Muslims do not easily stomach economic practices that trample on their faith. At a recent session in the Pakistan parliament, a member said at the tribune that it was permissible to charge interest in financial transactions. A tumult ensued, which was only calmed when the government agreed that Pakistan follow shariah law.

"The main points of Muslim economics," Huston Smith wrote, "cluster around the concern that the wealth of people be widely shared" (244). Islam does not oppose profit making or economic competition, but it insists that acquisitiveness and competition be "balanced by fair play and compassion." Islamic social law provides for the annual distribution of one fortieth of what one possesses to the poor (the Zakat). To hinder the accumulation of wealth in one person, the social law forbids primogeniture. The Quran says that inheritance must be divided among all children – daughters as well as sons. Islam also proclaims the principle that unearned money is not one's own. "This aims," Smith says, "at sleeping partners and all who live on inheritance without themselves contributing to society" (1958, 245).

Advocates of Islamic economics seek to "change contemporary society according to the vision [of their faith]" (Haneef and Amin, 2008, 1). The problem is that it has proven to be extremely difficult in Islamic departments of economics and finance to merge Islamic economics, with its highly moral tenets taken from Islam's sacred writings and shariah law, with Western neoclassical economics, which is based on amoral formal logic. If modernization means abandoning Islam in order to reconcile economic teaching with Western views, many Muslims prefer to find a third way that makes economics conform to Islam's moral code, no matter how "unscientific" Westerners proclaim the educational outcome.

Confucianism

In China, Buddhism tends to consider a God unimportant and Confucianism is not a religion but a philosophy of life. Therefore, most ethnic (Han) Chinese had no compelling transcendental reason to make religion the basis of a moral order. Besides, in our times the Communist Party officially turned its back on the country's feudal past in favor of socialist ideas about historical materialism imported from the Marxist West. Mao's faction felt so strongly about the issue that during the Cultural Revolution, Red Guards leveled a temple built in honor of Kong Fuzi (Confucius) in his home town of Qufu, in order to erase popular memories of the venerable teacher of ethics.

Even if the Communist intent has been to build a just society without religion, the grinding poverty that resulted from inherited demographic pressures forced the Party to make unjust compromises. The greatest divided rural from urban areas in the socialist system. The countryside, where 900 million plus people lived (80 percent of the population), was left to itself. Villagers could not migrate to the cities without official permission. The state-supported social welfare system that the Party organized covered 300 million people living in urban areas. They were the privileged in a deeply divided society, for only workers in state-governed enterprises obtained complete social security: old age and health insurance, accident insurance, disability insurance, pre-natal and maternity care, and survivor benefits (Wesner, 2005).

Sitting on a demographic volcano where the rural masses had been left out, in a society where corruption was rife, the Communist Party did an educational about-face. They not only returned to their traditions in moral philosophy to find the compass for moral order that they were now increasingly convinced historical materialism could not give them, but more and more they accepted the views of their erstwhile ethnic Chinese enemies, flourishing on the periphery of the Asian mainland, who attributed their success to Asian Values.

Annoyed US critics claim that Asian Values is too vague and self-contradictory a concept (there are many quite different values in Asia) to replace egocentric market-driven explanations for economic success in West Pacific Rim countries (Singapore, Hong Kong, Taiwan, and South Korea). But many ethnic Chinese do not easily dismiss the idea. Yadong Luo's study about Chinese interpersonal relationships (*guanxi*), draws the appropriate comparative definitional distinctions:

> Because of the heavy influence of Confucianism, Chinese often view themselves as interdependent with the surrounding social context. The self in relation to the other becomes the focus of individual experience. The view of an interdependent self is in sharp contrast to the Western view of an independent self. The latter sees each human being as an independent, self-contained and autonomous entity, who (a) comprises a unique configuration of internal attributes ... and (b) behaves primarily as a consequence of these internal attributes. (Luo, 2000, 8)

The Chinese view of self as interdependent with the surrounding social context "has implications for a variety of basic psychological processes ... and may be one of the most fundamental differences between the East and the West in social relations" (Luo, 2000, 8). People draw on the interdependent outlook to develop economic models about Asian Values, models pushed in the recent past by the prime ministers of Malaysia (Mahathir Mohammad) and Singapore (Lee Kuan Yew). Their view has had legs – witness the Harvard Forum on "Confucianism and Economic Development" in 2000, whose agenda's bibliography numbered 55 items.

To break out of the mass poverty impasse, the Chinese Communist Party decided in 1992 partially to abandon the central-command-state-managed enterprise system for some aspects of market-driven capitalism that it hoped would rapidly increase economic wealth. Whereas Chairman Mao had denigrated American managerialism, the new leadership decided to exploit US business school knowhow in order to develop the executive talent that successful operations in world markets demand. *Business Week* reported on the new educational pragmatism:

> The colossal effort by the central government of China to educate the nation's next generation of managers is unprecedented, and it has been undertaken at a speed that is nothing short of breathtaking. In just 15 years, Chinese B-schools raced through the evolution it took US B-schools more than half a century to accomplish – not by reinventing the wheel but by adopting the US model wholesale. (*Business Week*, January 9, 2006, 1)

Nonetheless, the Party decidedly did not adopt the US model "wholesale." The government (with the full knowledge that, as David Schweikert puts it, "things can fall apart, that large-scale worker or peasant societies can explode ...") looked to China's rich heritage in moral philosophy to prevent the explosion from happening, a heritage that stiffened the moral tenor of interpersonal relations (Schweikert, 2005, 11).

The regime found the compass for moral order for the most part in Confucianism. Kong Fuzi, born in 551 BC, formulated his ethical views in a time of war and disorder after the collapse of the Chou dynasty (Smith, 1958, 160). Chaotic historical circumstances led him to contemplate the connection between morality and social order, something the Communists are thinking about in China at the beginning of the twenty-first century.

The Master concluded that in early, simpler societies, people's inherited beliefs maintained social harmony. He called these spontaneous traditions collectively the "cake of custom" (Smith, 1958, 179). When the "cake of custom" crumbles, and it inevitably will as societies evolve, disorder ensues. Kong Fuzi asserted that when this happens, traditional beliefs would not restore themselves "spontaneously," but governments could develop and teach a body of "Deliberate Custom" – a consciously derived system of moral education – appropriate to the time, one that could establish a homeostasis between the expression of free will in individuals and a consciousness of their interpersonal rights and duties in society, and to state authority. Upon this homeostasis the survival of flourishing civilizations depended. The moral education that Kong Fuzi devised governed the individual as a social or relational being. On the societal level, it espoused "harmony" based on a two-way flow of duties, the people's duty of work for the development of the state ... balanced by the government's duty to care for the people and to provide for their welfare.

Kong Fuzi's rehabilitation began officially in 2001, when the Party for the first time sponsored his birthday celebration in Qufu. In September of the following year, state-controlled television broadcast festivities surrounding his 2,556th birthday on a scale never before seen in China. More than 2,500 people, including many fairly high-ranking members of the Communist Party cadre, journeyed to the philosopher's birthplace in Shandong province. In March 2006, President Hu Jintau proclaimed "Eight Do's and Don'ts" – moral guidelines for the Chinese people that were clearly Confucian-inspired: "Love, do not harm the Motherland, Serve, don't disserve the people, Uphold science, don't be ignorant and unenlightened, Work hard, don't be lazy and hate work, Be united and help each other, don't gain benefits at the expense of others, Be honest and trustworthy, no profit-mongering at the expense of your values, Be disciplined and law-abiding instead of chaotic and lawless, and Know plain living and hard struggle, do not wallow in luxuries and pleasures" (Crowell, 2005, 1).

In 2001 Renmin University (the first to do so on the Chinese mainland) erected a giant statue of Confucius – with the Ministry of Education's blessing. The next year the same university set up a Confucius Research Institute in a new College of National Studies, dedicated to the teaching of "National Learning" (*Guóxuê*): Confucianism, philosophy, history, and literature. Beijing Normal University Professor Yu Dan moved the Confucian revival from the classroom to the broader public with the publication of her book *Yu Dan's Reflection on "The Analects*," a compilation of seven lectures given on *The Lecture Room*, a popular prime-time show on China's CCTV 10. The book sold 4.2 million official and 6 million pirated copies in just a few months (Melvin, 2007, 1).

The government intended the Confucian revival to serve the needs of contemporary China by providing a humanist base upon which people could build within the nation and spread the glories of Chinese civilization abroad. To accomplish the latter the Ministry of Education, in partnership with receptive foreign governments, launched a program to create a global network of "Confucius Institutes" to teach the Chinese language and civilization. This "soft power" offensive offered the world an example of a modern peaceful "harmonious society," rather than "hard power" expansion by military force or economic conquest.

President Islam Karimov of Uzbekistan officially opened the first Confucius Institute in his country in June 2004. Three years later, Premier Wen Jiabao and the Portuguese premier signed an agreement to open one at the University of Lisbon. In these three years 128 Confucius Institutes came into existence: 46 in Asia, 46 in Europe, 26 in North America, 6 in Africa, and 4 in Oceania. At the end of 2010, the government had established 322 Confucius Institutes and 369 Confucius Classrooms in 96 countries.

The rapid growth of the American MBA business school education in China that *Business Week* reported has not undermined Chinese civilization. New MBA schools culturally adhere to Confucianism and National Learning. The connection is sometimes expressed in nomenclature, as in the name of the Shandong Confucian Business School. But if not, all the business schools have ethics courses rooted in Chinese moral philosophy's emphasis on social situational ethics, for example, in courses on "Confucius and Humanity" at the Cheung Kong Graduate School of Business in Beijing and in Shanghai, or in the Centre for Asian Entrepreneurship and Business Values and the business school at Hong Kong University.

Ambitious Chinese leaders want to make the Middle Kingdom the center of a thriving, world-connected, Asian economy in which management education, based on Chinese traditions of moral philosophy, will hold an important place (Bouée, 2010). Students from Taiwan, South Korea, Singapore, and even Japan attend China's increasingly viable business schools because they feel cultivating interpersonal relationships in them is the key to their individual economic futures. Mainland Chinese, too, increasingly study in their own country – sometimes forgoing chances to enter management schools in Europe and America – for the same reasons ("More Taiwanese," 2002; Yeh, 2007). People are not naïve about society's need for entrepreneurial energy, but that is not lacking in the Chinese people. For balance, they need an ethic of harmony to give their densely populated society time to increase the economic pie to the point where most Chinese can escape grinding poverty.

If the liberal credo Croce enunciated served and serves as a moral precept for democratic capitalism and management, it cannot serve as one in the era of a globalizing management caste. But without such a compass, Western capitalism is deprived of the moral force that has always underpinned its expansion. Historic religions have stepped into the moral vacuum to reassert themselves as a force against morally spent managerialism; non-Western people turn to them for solutions to modern problems that managerialism cannot give them, thereby compounding the decline of the West.

Christian morality, the feudal heritage, and codetermination in Germany

German sociologists in the nineteenth century distinguished between the German concept of *Gemeinschaft* (community) and the West European and American concept of *Gesellschaft* (society). Another view that is not as familiar in the UK and the US is the distinction made between the entity and the proprietary conception of the firm (Moores and Steadman, 1986). The components of the entity idea of the firm are the capitalist owners (the individual capitalist or family proprietors in the small firms, the stockholders in the large, publicly traded corporations), the employees, who collectively constitute the firm's knowhow and skills and as such are as integral a part of the firm as the capitalists who fund it, and the firm's clients or customers, who pay for the services and products that the firm generates. The great difference between this entity and the proprietary model extant in Britain and America is that in the entity, the so-called Rhineland Model, the employees are legally empowered to participate in the firm's governance. And they do so through employee representation on German supervisory boards and in employee-elected works councils that are actively involved in firm governance. The proprietary model, on the other hand, excludes, *de jure*, employees from the firm's governance, which is the exclusive right that the owners delegate to management. If employees participate in the firm's governance it is at management's discretion. And the US management caste frowns on such participation.

Two points need to be made about codetermination with respect to moral order. First, the idea of employee participation is rooted in nineteenth-century German corporatism (the *Ständestaat*) and bureaucratic legalism. It gained respectability in the Second Empire (1871–1918), when Emperor Wilhelm II, an autocrat in a reformist mood, in a speech in 1890 asked for the creation of worker-representative bodies within factories that could defend employees' legitimate interests, within a corporate body, in negotiations with employers. The resulting Law for the Protection of Labor granted the workers joint consultation rights (*Mitberatungsrecht*) on social matters. This was not codetermination (*Mitbestimmung*), but the law authorized the organization of plant committees in all factories covered by the Industrial Code of 1869, with more than twenty employees. It required management to issue and abide by shop regulations spelling out relations with workers. Germans like to state relationships in detail. In other words, it was the autocratic-bureaucratic Bismarckian state that the historians called anachronistic, not a liberal-democratic regime, that started Germany on the path to its current system of participatory management and welfarism.

But there was nothing inevitable about the institutionalization of codetermination in its current form; its fate in twentieth-century Germany depended on unpredictable and unimagined if not random events. As the semi-autocratic monarchy fell to pieces in the chaos of defeat in 1918, employee participation in management took a big step forward. Employers in the revolutionary month of November 1918 capitulated almost entirely to union pressures. Fearing Bolshevism, their associations signed collective agreements, which would not have been possible before World War One, that gave employees rights of codetermination with management in social policy and obligated management to consult employee representatives in personnel and economic decision-making. The July 1919 socialist-liberal-progressive majority in the Constituent Assembly subsequently wrote codetermination into the Weimar Constitution: Article 165 called for "the equal participation" of blue- and white-collar workers (*Arbeiter* and *Angestellte*) in the economic development of production forces.

Events intervened in the form of National Socialism to undo these measures. Hitler believed in the leader principle and acted accordingly. When Germany climbed out of the rubble in 1945 after the Twelve-Year Reich, shamed by the complicity of the country's business and industrial leadership with Nazism, and even more humiliated by the depravity of the regime, codetermination took on renewed life. After the founding of the Federal Republic of Germany, the legislature passed a Codetermination

Law for the Iron and Steel Industry (1951) and, the following year, a Works Constitution Act. This legislation did not give employees equal rights of codetermination with management in the governance of companies, but, as strengthened in subsequent legislation, it did offer them very extensive rights of codetermination in large firms. Fifty years later, codetermination is part of Germany's industrial way of life.

The adoption of codetermination in Germany was a unique event rooted in the specificity of German history. Powerful labor unions and the Social Democratic Party backed the legislation. But that does not explain why these laws passed. Without the conservatives under Konrad Adenauer (the German Christian Democrats and the German Christian Union) and the support of Catholic and Protestant church leaders all over the country, the legislation would never have been adopted. In 2005, the German Chancellor Angela Merkel acknowledged the affiliation between codetermination and Christian moral order. Addressing the Christian Democratic Party faithful, she said that the German

> Social Market Economy, in which codetermination is embedded, concretized the Christian view of man. It is a social and economic order created by Conrad Adenauer and Ludwig Ehard. It arose from the Catholic social teaching and the Protestant ethic that was then brought into reality as a practical model. (Merkel, 2005; also see Klüber, 1977)

In the codetermination laws, German religious conservatives sought moral redemption, by punishing the corporate managerial elite that had soiled itself though collaboration with the Nazi dictatorship in its crimes against humanity, and by rendering justice to workers and their unions, who had often been the Nazis' victims.

The moral basis of US managerialism post World War Two

Few Americans saw codetermination that way. General Lucius Clay, who headed the occupation authority in the US Zone after the war, stymied German efforts to introduce codetermination modes of management in German business when Germans assumed increasing control over their civil government in the late 1940s. The American High Commissioner, John J. McCloy, was not neutral about German efforts in the Bundestag to create codetermination in the German Federal Republic. Although recognizing Germany's right to decide the issue for itself, he told German trade unionists not to be surprised if Americans refused to invest in companies co-managed by workers. This was a not-too-subtle pressure against the legislation's enactment.

US private business for its part openly opposed the introduction of codetermination in Germany. Getting wind of the proposed German legislation, the National Association of Manufacturers sent a delegation to Europe led by Eldridge Haines to lobby against the bill. Gordon Michler, head of the German Committee in the American National Foreign Trade Council, joined the transatlantic sojourn to speak against it. In the US a representative of the National Association of Manufacturers wrote an open letter to the German Council in New York, published in the *New York Times*, warning that Americans would not invest in German industry if the codetermination bill passed (Locke, 1996, 64–67).

Sometimes the Americans stated, as in the *New York Times* article, that codetermination was a "new socialism in the relations between capitalism and labor." But usually, taking a proprietary viewpoint, they just stressed that codetermination robbed stockholders of their right of control. When the Social Democrats–Liberal coalition in the mid 1970s strengthened employee participation in company governance, Americans again protested. Henry Ford III, visiting his company's factories in Cologne at the time of the debate in the Bundestag, deplored the new legislation's infringement on the prerogatives of management (reported in *New York Times*, October 17, 1975).

But the management caste running American corporations did not consider itself, nor was it considered postwar, a bunch of unprincipled ruffians. Definitions of managerialism usually pointed out at the time that managers, although their fiduciary duty was to stockholders, had the moral duty to look after the well-being of other stakeholders in the firm and to be good corporate citizens. The post-1945 version of managerialism, moreover, cobbled together elements of a partnership between the management caste, big labor, and government first hammered out during the New Deal and World War Two. Heralded collective bargaining agreements provided for better wages and working conditions; they introduced company retirement plans, medical plans, and other social benefits. Between 1948 and 1953, an Inter-University Labor Relations Program sponsored the publication of a significant academic literature on industrial relations. These monographs, written by industrial labor relations people who were soon to be renowned (Clark Kerr, Frederick Harbison, John Dunlop, Charles Meyer, and others), emphasized "the extension of democracy in industry through collective bargaining permitting both sides of industry ... to mold good relations" (Carew, 1987, 56).

Well might George Meany, of the AFL-CIO, have reasoned in 1951: "Where you have a well-established industry and a well-established union, you are going to get to the point where a strike doesn't make sense" (Bell, 1951, 86). And well might Walter Reuther, the head of the United Auto Workers, after reaching agreement in 1950 with management at General Motors, have echoed that the five-year contract, which called for an annual wage increase, pegged on anticipated productivity gains, cushioned against inflation by a cost-of-living bonus, was truly historic.

More significantly, after World War Two, for the general public the success of the country's core corporations and the well-being of individual citizens seemed for the first time in US history inextricably bound. This environment converted the sharpest critics of management to pro-management stances. David Lilienthal, a former New Deal planner, in a 1953 book *Big Business: A New Era*, expressed the sentiments of the American people, the vast majority of whom, in a public opinion poll that same year, approved of big business. The gap between rich and poor closed. The share of national income of the top 1 percent of income earners fell from 19 percent in 1914 to 7.7 percent in 1946. By the mid 1940s, almost half of all American families fell comfortably within the middle-income group (Reich, 1992, 49). Although there remained plenty of dissenters, because of these achievements US managerialism cemented a bond of trust between the management caste and the American people based on material success.

Never in their sweetest liberal dreams, however, did the managerial caste think of sharing governance with employees or with labor in a regime of codetermination.

The breakup of moral order after 1980

Trust and moral order, however, cannot easily be maintained if the material basis for them evaporates. With the dramatic decline or extinction of so many mass production American industries in the 1980s (cars, rubber, steel, machine tools, electrical and electronic appliances, etc.), the economic base of heavily unionized mass production industries shrank. Economists and management scientists explain what happened in neutral analytical terms, but in human terms the facts are that stockholders colluded with the management caste to maldistribute the diminishing wealth in their favor. The gap between the rich and poor started to grow and has increased steadily for thirty years. Managers and their corporate lawyers working to achieve maldistribution of the shrinking economic pie in their favor dissolved the social pact on which the previous trust rested. The oft-told story of promises to employees and unions broken by management is legend now – of downsizing, of outsourcing in order to cut the cost of wages and benefits, of chapter eleven bankruptcies that permitted management to set aside union contracts, of management raiding employee pension funds, etc. Management, employees, and stockholders could have opted to share the pain, but the management caste in charge of American corporations squeezed powerless employees hard. Any idea of a moral order under managerialism disappeared.

The US Christian revival and the issue of firms' governance

If it had been left to German corporate executives after World War Two, there never would have been much codetermination in the country. As it were, German Christians acted as the conscience of the nation to force on the German nation at the margin a new moral order in firms' governance. The American Christian community's attitude toward the management caste as it abandoned all semblance of social ethics in the treatment of nonmanagement employees after 1980 was the mirror opposite. To understand why requires a brief excursion into the story of American Christianity at the end of the twentieth century.

Max Weber after World War One argued that modernization inevitably resulted in the destruction of religion.

This "secularization theory" continued to be a prominent theme in the sociology of religion after 1945: in works by Ernst Troeltsch, Bryan Wilson, Thomas Luckmann, Peter L. Berger, Karel Dobbelaere, and others. They asserted that "religion's influence on all aspects of life – from personal habits to social institutions – is in dramatic decline. People have become and are becoming less religious" (Swatos and Christianos, 1991, 4). In the 1960s, one religious sociologist, A. F. C. Wallace, predicted the death of religion because "[it is doubtful] if modernity [can continue to] combine religious tradition with the overpowering impersonal features of our time: scientific research ..., high technology, multinational capitalism, bureaucratic life, and so on" (Swatos and Christianos, 1991, 4). "Governments," he predicted, would no longer turn to "priests, ministers, rabbis, and mullahs for expertise when solving world problems but to economists, physicists, and political scientists" (Swatos and Christianos, 1991, 3).

Proponents of secularization theory certainly were wrong. Religious belief strengthened at the end of the twentieth century. In 1991 Bill McKibben classified four out of every five Americans as Christian. "Every other statistic one can cite about American behavior is essentially also a measure of professed Christians. That's what America is, a place saturated in Christian identity" (McKibben, 2005, 7). The American Religious Identification Survey of 2000 tracked the growth, but it also registered significant shifts in the weight of Christian groupings. Between 1990 and 2000 the American population grew by 18 percent while the number of self-described Catholics increased by 14.5 percent (46,004,000 to 50,873,000). In the same period, people who referred to themselves as Protestants declined as a percentage of the US population. But within the Protestant category the relative size of groups changed (Table 2.1).

Table 2.1

Christianity in the USA

Principal denominations	1990	2000
Methodist/Wesleyan	14,174,000	14,150,000
Lutheran	9,110,000	9,580,000
Presbyterian	4,985,000	5,596,000
Episcopalian/Anglican	3,042,000	4,407,000
Salvation Army	27,000	25,000
Pentecostal/Charismatic	3,191,000	4,407,000
Evangelical	242,000	1,032,000

Source: Pew Research Center, *Americans Struggle with Religion's Role at Home and Abroad*. PEW Survey Report, 2000, 1–6.

Alan Wolfe also emphasized the story of stagnation and decline in mainline Protestant churches (Presbyterians, Episcopalians, etc.) (Wolfe, 2004, 103). Nationwide in the thirty years up to 2007, membership in Methodist, Lutheran, Presbyterian, and Episcopalian churches fell by one third. In certain regions the losses were worse. In the New York region 1,000 mainline Protestant churches, with a total membership at survey time of 300,000 parishioners, lost 45 percent of their membership between 1960 and 2004. Mainline Protestants slowly moved to white suburbia, while Pentecostal Charismatics and Evangelicals thrived in these fast-growing areas of affluence. The challenge to Christians to provide a social ethic appropriate to moral order depended a lot on the attitude of the new groups.

Since Christianity is a historical religion, much of what American Christians believe today is rooted in past events. The main events were the birth, life, death, and resurrection of Jesus Christ. American Christians' views on moral order can best be explained through referencing two of them. They are, first, the Resurrection and the effect it had on Christ's followers and, second, the events of Jesus's life, as recorded in the New Testament, and the effect that his teachings and deeds had on people.

The Resurrection

For Christians everywhere the Resurrection is the quintessential event. "Faith in the Resurrection," Huston Smith reminds us, "gave the impetus to the rise of the Apostolic Church and the Christology that supports it. The word that swept across the ancient world two thousand years ago was not Jesus' admonition to 'Love Thy Neighbor.' It was the Good News that Christ had Risen, and with it the implication that those who believed in Him could, like Him and with Him, triumph over sin and death to new life. It was irresistible" (Smith, 1958, 311).

This belief in salvation through Christ sparked a profound religious experience in often quite ordinary men and women. Smith relates that the Good News so infused the souls of early Christians that one could actually see, not just hear, that they loved one another and that an inner peace, an unspeakable but discernable glorious joy radiated from their faces, because "Life had ceased to be a problem to be solved" (Smith, 1958, 315). This spiritual joy unites Christians across the ages. It is seen in the born-again Evangelicals and Pentecostals (today the fastest-growing Christian denomination in the world), just as the ineffaceable joy could be seen in the appearance and behavior of first-generation Christians in Graeco-Rome ("A Survey on Religion," 2007, 4). For Christians the Resurrection is about what could be called the *Ultimate Egoism* – the promise that every individual shall have eternal life. This commitment to God for personal salvation is moving, but it does not provide a basis for social ethics.

Historical Jesus

If Christ's Crucifixion and Resurrection involve individuals in an ultimate ego trip, the Christian encounter with his sayings and knowledge of the events in his life let him/her witness Ultimate Selflessness. Smith talks about this in an extraordinary portrait of Jesus:

> Certainly the most impressive thing about the teachings of Jesus is not that he taught them but that he lived them. His entire life was one of complete humility, self-giving, and love which sought not its own. The supreme evidence of his humility ... is that it is impossible to discover precisely what Jesus thought of Himself. He was not concerned that men should know what He was. His concern was for people to know God and His will for their lives. By indirection this tells us something about what Jesus thought of Himself too; he thought infinitely less of Himself than he did of God. It is impossible to read what Jesus said about selflessness without sensing at once how free he Himself was of pride. (1958, 309)

Jesus was active in a time of considerable economic and social injustice – a time much like our own. In first-century Palestine, about two thirds of the wealth created by agriculture ended up in the hands of the urban elite. That left only one third for 90 percent of the population, the rural peasants who were the primary producers of wealth. Furthermore, the Temple was also a heavy drain on these peasants' resources (Borg, 1994, 102).

Jesus seems to have challenged the existing social order and to have offered an alternative. As the ultimate selfless person, Christ points to a way of living that improves, or at least attempts to improve, life on this planet. God expects Christians to care for the weak, the sick, the helpless, and the oppressed and to challenge injustice wherever it exists. In the prophetical literature of the Old Testament a number of passages clearly indicate that worship of the God of Israel must be combined with the fulfillment of moral obligations, not just of a personal nature but social obligations. Jesus continued and expanded this tradition. Unlike salvation (Ultimate Egoism), social justice (Ultimate Selflessness) is not a burning issue for American Christians in our time. In the Christian world, Bill McKibben reported in *Harper's Magazine*, the United States:

> ranked second to last, after Italy, among developed countries in government foreign aid. Per Capita we each provide fifteen cents a day in official development assistance to poor countries. And it's not because we were giving to private charities for relief work instead. Such funding increases our average daily donations by just six pennies, to twenty-one cents. It's also not because Americans were too busy taking care of their own; nearly 18% of Americans lived in poverty compared with, say, 8% in Sweden. In fact, by pretty much any measure of caring for the least among us – childhood nutrition, infant mortality, and access to pre-school – we come in nearly last among advanced nations and often by wide margins. (McKibben, 2005, 4)

Mainline Protestant churches and Catholics had a reputation for poverty relief, especially churches located in decaying inner cities, but the rapidly growing Pentecostal and Evangelical churches in the white Protestant suburbs did not. They focused on Ultimate Egoism not selflessness. And these new conservative Christians came to make up 25 percent of the American population compared to 20 percent in 1960 ("A Survey on Religion," 2007, 4).

The Pew Research Center reported after September 11, 2001 that 48 percent of Americans thought that the United States has had special protection from God for most of its history. Some 71 percent of the new conservative white Evangelical Protestants believe this, compared with just 40 percent of mainline Protestants. Moreover, 86 percent of white Evangelical Protestants (57 percent of white mainline Protestants and 58 percent of white Catholics) also believe that religious faith is at the core of America's strength (Pew Research Center, 2002, 2). The growth of white Evangelicals within the mix of the Protestant faithful not only reinforces ego-centered spiritual preoccupations, at the expense of concerns about social justice, but also intensifies efforts to "Christianize" the state. In 2004, 78 percent of Evangelical Christians voted for Bush, two thirds of whom favored Christians' expressing political views (only one third of white mainline Protestants did) (PEW, 2002). House Majority Leader Tom Delay, after hearing his pastor say that "the war between America and Iraq is the gateway to the Apocalypse," told the congregation and 225 Christian TV and radio stations on a national hookup: "Ladies and gentlemen, what has been spoken here is the truth of God" (McKibben 2005, 20).

Far more important to this study was the Christian Right's effort in partnership with the Republican Party to "baptize" the American system of managerialism. Or, as one Christian Conservative phrased it, "The evangelicals' defense of freedom is so strong that they regard labor unions as antithetical to the culture of enterprise that makes America great" (Hart, 2007, 1).

These Christians sometimes also oppose ideas about redistribution of wealth through progressive taxation (something German Christians, out of a sense of social solidarity, approve). The Christian Coalition of America – founded in 1989 in order to "preserve, protect and defend the Judeo-Christian values that made this the greatest country in history" – proclaimed in 2005 that "top of its legislative agenda would be the making permanent of President Bush's 2001 federal tax cuts," which primarily favored the rich (McKibben, 2005, 13; McGarvey, 2004).

In Alabama, where 90 percent of the people call themselves Christians, the state ranks forty-eighth out of fifty in the amount of state and local tax monies gathered, most of which come from a super-regressive sales tax. In order to solve a fiscal crisis and to improve the state's school systems, which routinely ranks with America's worst, the governor proposed to raise property taxes. Some 68 percent of Christians voted against the measure. The Christian Coalition of Alabama joined the wealthiest in opposition. John Giles, the group's president, stated "you'll find most Alabamans have a charitable heart; they just don't want it coming out of their pockets." The group's website proclaimed "that progressive taxation results in punishing success [and that] when an individual works for income, that money belongs to the individual" (McKibben, 2005, 213).

Recent surveys show that three quarters of the American people believe that the expression "God helps those who help themselves" can be found in the Holy Scriptures, when in fact it originates with Benjamin Franklin (McKibben, 2005, 15).

If American Christians, with Evangelicals in the lead, oppose so many social programs (Medicare, social security, etc.), what do their pastors and priests actually do after the sermonizing is over? Those in the mainline Protestant, Catholic, and Evangelical churches do Jesus's work; they tend the flock. Much of this is important personally – marriage counseling, dealing with delinquents, consoling grieving families after a death, etc. As for their parishioners, what they do depends very much on where they live. If they live in inner cities, they are very much preoccupied with poverty and blight. But if they are suburbanites, removed from the inner cities, their religious life reflects the values of the shopping mall. A *New York Times* reporter, visiting one of the new mega-churches outside Phoenix, Arizona, found a "drive-through latte stand, Crispy Crème doughnuts at every service, and sermons about 'how to discipline your children, how to invest your money, and how to reduce your debt'" (McKibben, 2005, 15).

Bestsellers on the Christian Booksellers' list for middle-class Christians included Joel Osteen's *Your Best Life Now* (2005), which *Publishers' Weekly* called "a treatise on how to get God to serve the demands of self-centered individuals," Beth Moore's *Believing God* (2004), which asks whether we are living as fully as we can, and Dr. Gary Chapman's *The Five Love Languages* (2004), which discusses how to communicate with "your significant other" (McKibben, 2005, 15). The reporter concluded that this Christian book list is hardly distinguishable from a secular list of bestsellers "with its fixation on self-improvement, on self-esteem, on self." The Christian books "offer too uncanny a reflection of the dominant secular culture [created by market-driven late twentieth century American capitalism], a culture of unrelenting self-obsession" (McKibben, 2005, 15).

No doubt, comparing these popular comments about the Evangelical and Pentecostal movement to those of Confucius, Islamic scholars, and German professors of theology is like comparing apples with oranges. Nor do the comparisons take into consideration the serious critique of US managerialism in the United States by theologians such as John B. Cobb, Jr. and his colleagues in the Process Theology movement (Cobb, 1980, 2007, 2009a, 2009b). But the ability of the religious Right to affect politics in America and thereby public policy makes their views especially important.

We are not saying that conservative Christians have no social conscience about the plight of less fortunate citizens in America, nor that they necessarily oppose social programs. To say this would be patent nonsense. But we are saying that conservative American Protestants, unlike German Christians, did not adopt an organic conception of the firm, with employee participation in firm governance as a featured element, and, therefore, that they did not oppose in any significant way the growth of managerialism in America and often promoted it. Moreover, from a purely structural perspective, US Christianity's relationship with secular management was the opposite of what occurred in Germany. There, theology influenced firm governance through codetermination; in the US, secular management influenced religion, for not only did conservative US Christians usually dislike trade unionism and reject schemes of employee participation and therewith accept the "oppression" of employees in Simone Weil's sense, but they fell under the influence of managerialism and business school educational models in their own operations. The rapid growth of mega-churches made them susceptible to administrative-organizational problems like any growing organization and, therefore, susceptible to dominant secular management theories propagated in business schools. In 1991 a case study prepared for the Harvard Business School, by Leonard Schlesinger and James Mellado, pointed out that churches were badly managed and could get a bigger bang for their bucks and raise more of them by using management techniques and thinking that had been developed in business schools (Schlesinger and Mellado, 1991). In 2007, Harvard Business School professor Michael Porter, in "Doing Well at Doing Good," pushed the agenda of managerialism on churches by suggesting that they could learn a lot in strategic thinking and operational management from business schools (Porter, 2007).

Academia and business school education

If the moral conscience of US managers could not be ameliorated by the guiding hand of a resurgent American Christianity, neither could it be improved through interaction with the reformed business schools. That interaction can best be explained by describing the evolution of humanistic studies within the university community in which the reformed business schools took their place. The story is told under four rubrics: (1) how the long conflict between science and the humanities, the "two cultures," as C. P. Snow called them in a famous lecture in 1959, affected ethical education in the university, (2) how students fled the humanities for the disciplines of the new paradigm as the century wore on, (3) how the postmodernist attack on sciences taught in the universities ended up diminishing the standing of the humanities instead, and (4) how universities and business schools turned into money mills.

The two cultures

In the early nineteenth century the study of economic management was called "political economy," and before that it was part of moral philosophy and theology. Amartya Sen, in *On Ethics and Economics*, traces economics in ancient Greece to ethics (quoted in Mofid, 2005, 1). Aristotle raised ethical questions two thousand years ago, when he made the distinction between *oikonomikos* (household trading), "which he approved of and thought essential to the workings of any even moderately complex society" (Mofid, 2005, 26), and *chrematisike* (the art of getting rich), which he condemned because it entailed trade for profit. Over a thousand years later, in the Christian Middle Ages, scholars continued to use the language of ethics, when, for instance, they discussed what was regarded as just and right and for the common good in economic matters.

The struggle to remove the moral dimension from "scientific" subjects really began two hundred years ago. Robert N. Bellah observed that Immanuel Kant drew a clear distinction between the cognitive and the ethical, between, in Kant's terms, pure reason and practical reason. According to him, an unbridgeable gap separates the two realms. Since we cannot get to one from the other, each must operate in its own sphere.

The English economists took it from there, but the renunciation of ethical concerns did not come abruptly. Like most eighteenth-century Enlightenment philosophers, Adam Smith, as Enteman's study clearly shows, was very much preoccupied with morality when he wrote *The Wealth of Nations* (Enteman, 1993). But late-nineteenth-century neoclassical economists tried to turn the subject into an academic discipline, rooted in a cognitive science, which banished ethics from a discipline that people began simply to call "economics." To affirm its supposed scientific character, its creators mapped the neoclassical economic model onto Newtonian mechanics.

Stanley Jevons, inventor with Karl Menger of marginal utility analysis, described their scientific goal: "all branches and divisions of economic science must be pervaded by certain general principles. It is to the investigation of such principles – to the tracing out of the mechanics of self-interest and utility, that [economics] is devoted" (Jevons, quoted in Fullbrook, 2003, 2).

Fullbrook describes how the architects of neoclassical economics aligned their new discipline isomorphically with Newtonian mechanics:

> In Neoclassical economics, 'bodies' translates 'individuals' or agents,' 'motions' translates 'exchange of goods,' 'forces' translates 'desires' or 'preferences,' which when summed become 'supply and demand,' 'mechanical equilibrium' becomes 'market equilibrium,' this being when the difference between supply and demand is zero, and 'physical systems' translates 'markets.' ... All exchanges were said to magically take place at the prices that equated demand and supply. (Fullbrook, 2003, 2)

Since a viable science had to be expressed mathematically, neoclassical economics did as well. By the nineteenth century, mathematicians had started to work in social science. In 1854 George Boole (1815–64) in *An Investigation of the Laws of*

Thought used mathematics to analyze the logic of language, and Léon Walras mathematized economics. With this achievement he stated, in his *Elements of Pure Economics,* that economics had become a "science, which resembles the physico-mathematical sciences in every respect" (Fullbrook, 2003, 2).

The problem is that mathematized neoclassical economics did not resemble "the physico-mathematical sciences in every respect." It did not in fact resemble them at all. Here the issue is not deficiencies in knowledge – that was covered in Chapter 1 – but what the triumph of neoclassical economics meant for the existence of moral order.

As the "value free" cognitive-based management sciences developed in business schools, in departments of industrial administration, and in economics, the people in humanities scarcely at first noticed. Their subject, the spirit of man, had nothing to do with game theory, linear programming, and the like. Moreover, the humanities always prided themselves on the vital function they played in American universities and liberal arts colleges. If two cultures existed in the 1950s, the people in the humanities felt that theirs would always remain an important part of higher education because of the moral dimension's importance to humanity.

They could in fact trace their educational purpose to religious roots and to the great classical innovators in history. One of the more influential, Wilhelm von Humboldt, had carried out a thorough reform of Prussian secondary and university education at the beginning of the nineteenth century. His reforms stamped Prussian-German education with humanist values for over one hundred years. Many felt, especially before World War One, that Humboldt's reformed institutions, much like the public schools in Victorian Britain, gave the leadership cadres the moral instruction that underpinned national achievement.

Humboldt wished to use classical languages as media for the

cultivation of this "inner self" not just to educate the individual but to prepare an entire ruling class for its leadership function, specifically in his time and place, the Prussian civil servants (*Beamte*). He considered the *Beamtentum*, to which he belonged, to be a general class, charged in the Prussian kingdom with looking after the public interest – not a special-interest group, like businessmen, that pursued its own selfish interests (Wertz, 1993). To carry out this task the *Beamte* needed character more than cognitive knowledge. Humboldt expected a classical education in *Gymnasien* (secondary schools) to help instill in the youth of the directing classes a sense of honor, honesty, duty, and patriotism as well as a deep appreciation of culture, before they set off to the university to learn the cognitive subjects (mostly law at the time) needed to carry out administrative functions. *Bildung* (education) was first, then *Ausbildung* (training).

Although peculiarly Prussian, Humboldt's reform did not differ in intent much from the reigning educational philosophies of people running the English public schools, the French *lycées* and *collèges*, and private American liberal arts colleges. They could not have known that in the second half of the twentieth century one of the two cultures within the edifice of higher education would wither away and, with it, the vision of morality.

Fleeing the humanities

In 1992, Robert B. Reich described the recent transformation of the US labor market. He separated market demand into three categories of activity: "routine production services, in person services, and symbolic analytic services." The third grouping is the significant one. People dispensing them amounted in the early 1990s to 20 percent of the labor force. They were college graduates for the most part, highly in demand because their skills could solve, identify, and broker problems by manipulating symbols. Research scientists, design engineers, software engineers, civil engineers, biotechnology engineers, sound engineers, investment bankers, management consultants, financial consultants, armament consultants, strategic planners, management information specialists, marketing strategists, and more. (Reich, 1992, 210)

They were the minions of "the new paradigm" in management education. Because they earned the high salaries, the gap between their incomes and the incomes of those working in the other two services constantly grew, and irreversibly so, in the money-oriented US capitalist employment system.

American college students are inordinately practical people. They know where the good jobs are and they know the kind of education needed to get them. In the education marketplace, they are the consumers who determine the source of supply. They started to shun the humanities. Near the century's end (1998), James Engell and Anthony Dangerfield, in the *Harvard Magazine*, reported that "the humanities represent a sharply declining proportion of all undergraduate degrees" (Engell and Dangerfield, 1998). Between 1970 and 1994, the number of bachelor's degrees in computer and information sciences, police and protective services, and transportation and moving materiel increased fivefold, in health professions and public administration threefold, and in business administration twofold (from a high 1970 plateau). In English, foreign languages, philosophy, religion, and history, the number of bachelor's degrees awarded registered absolute declines. Humanities in some universities are being eliminated (Fish, 2010; Harris, 2010).

The postmodernist fight

Not that an intense, decades-long struggle against modernism did not happen in higher education. The famous postmodernist challenge by its very name strongly opposed the new paradigm in management education. But it missed its mark.

Like Marx, postmodernists stand Enlightenment rhetoric on its head in order the better to attack it. Whereas Marx talked about how the bourgeoisie created a superstructure of thought and moral teachings to protect its interests, the postmodernists discuss how dominant groups construct authoritative meta-narratives that ignore the life experience of the disadvantaged – women, slaves, minorities, nonwhites, and generally the poor – and leave the fact of their exploitation hidden, that is, until the postmodernists deconstruct the rhetoric of the dominant dialogue.

Since the new management paradigm is modernism par excellence, the rhetoric it employs is a prime example of what postmodernists are talking about. When the neoclassical economist states that "demand for labor varies inversely to wages," he uses "neutral analytical" language, a principle of economics. When he adds another principle, that "labor is most effectively utilized when workers compete in a free job market," he uses a meta-narrative of the dominant capitalist class, which obscures the fact that these principles send actual working people on a race to the bottom in their competition with each other. If the scientist invents a mathematical model of general equilibrium or rational choice theory in order to acquire prescriptive rigor, he continues the meta-narrative of dominance under the guise of neutral mathematical functions. Or, if neoclassical economists develop an "infinite growth model," which purports to "show how and why it is possible for production and consumption to grow forever," and that model ignores the ecosystem, then their scientific language harms the environmental interests of mankind. It turned out, then, that the new paradigm in management studies did not abolish ethical considerations but only obscured them.

The problem is that the postmodernist attack on positivism had unintended results because it weakened the position of the humanities in universities more than it did science, technology, and the new paradigm in business schools. The postmodernist critique originated in philosophy and linguistics; it is and has always been preoccupied with language, with deconstruction of texts, not with mathematics, natural science, or engineering. It mounted a determined attack primarily in the humanities – in history, in philosophy, in literary criticism, in religious studies, and in other liberal arts – confidence in the moral educational value of which were deeply shaken by the force of the critique. But science, technology, and business studies – the real modernists' disciplines – have not been shaken a bit by the postmodernist movement.

Postmodernism undoubtedly ended the authoritative narrative (Lyotard) in the humanities when it introduced new voices into the dialogue, but it also, inadvertently perhaps, weakened the humanities within the university. It has been, its critics in the humanities say, a negative if not destructive force because it has torn down the Enlightenment project without putting any ethical norms in its place. Its critique of the humanities amounts to "an unjustified betrayal of the modernist project of building an ever better world" (Beyer, 2006, 2).

The money mills

Does this mean that Humboldt's vision was wrong? Not according to people in the humanities. For them the problem arises not so much from the expansion within the academy of empirical science and technology at the expense of the humanities. The problem does not even come from science's methodological lack of concern for ethics. The issue is not science and technology but scientists, engineers, and business students

– whole people. Robert Bellah observed that when we speak of someone as a "true scholar or a true scientist," we mean that the person has a "character or a stance towards the world that is clearly normative or ethical, not merely cognitive" (2000, 1). He speaks of the scientists' and scholars' need for "judgment" as well as cognitive skill in their work. Bellah uses "judgment" in an elevated sense:

> One could say ... that judgment is the most intellectual of the practical virtues and the most practical of the intellectual virtues. [It] in this use of the term involves a sense of proportion, of larger meaning, of what a situation requires, at once cognitively and ethically. [When we say that an action or a person is] truly human we mean simultaneously that this person is such as a human can be and such as he ought to be. (Bellah, 2000, 3)

Here Bellah touches on Aristotle's notion of final cause, i.e., what is science for? The answer is ethical, the good of mankind. It is a mistake to believe that those who practice it do not need moral character as well as verbal, mathematical, and problem-solving skills. The traditional university had liberal arts as a central part of its core precisely because "the university has never been a place devoted solely to the function of character or to pure inquiry." For the balance that society needs, it has had both.

Humanists complain that big government and big business have, through their hookup with the new teaching and research paradigm in universities, turned these institutions into money markets. They could have added that managerialism in university governance itself promotes this invasion (Baldridge, 1971; Child, 1982, 2007). The authors of the *Harvard Magazine* piece about the decline of the humanities concur:

> When we termed the last thirty years the Age of Money, we were in part referring to the dollar influx [into the universities] of research grants, higher tuition, and grander capital improvements.

But there's another, more symbolic, aspect to the Age of Money, and one not less powerful for being more symbolic. The mere concept of money turns out to be the secret key to 'prestige,' influence, and power in the American academic world. (quoted in Bellah, 2000, 6)

It turns out at the end of the twentieth century that the issue for higher education is not science versus the humanities but science/humanities versus money/managerialism.

The most successful university disciplines, Bellah argues, have to offer: (1) a promise of money ("The field is popularly linked ... to improved chances of securing an occupation or profession that promises above-average lifetime earnings."); (2) a knowledge of money ("The field itself studies money, whether practically or more theoretically, i.e., fiscal, business, financial and/or economic matters and markets."); (3) a source of money ("The field receives significant external money, i.e., research contracts, federal grant or funding support, or corporate underwriting."). If this portrayal is right, Bellah affirms, "then our life together in the university is governed by neither the intellectual nor the moral virtues but by a vice, namely, cupidity, acquisitiveness, or just plain avarice" (Bellah, 2000, 6; see also Amadae and de Mesquita, 1999; Amadae, 2003).

Perhaps more important, for humanists, the content of the subjects studied and the mathematized methodologies devised to study them reinforce the development of the plutocratic university. Bellah particularly singles out Rational Choice Theory (RCT) (Amadae and de Mesquita, 1999; McCumber, 2001). "In America, and to some degree throughout the world," he observes,

we seem to have returned in the past thirty years to something from the last decades of the nineteenth century, that is, unconstrained laissez-faire capitalism. And just as the theory of social Darwinism mirrored the strident capitalism of the late nineteenth century, so the rise of Rational Choice Theory reflects the emergence of neo-laissez-faire capitalism in the last thirty years. (Bellah, 2000, 6)

RCT is taught to students as "scientific truth." "Every year 1.4 million undergraduates in the US," Neva Goodwin, co-director of the Global Development and Environment Institute at Tufts University, affirmed in 2003, "take an introduction to economics course that teaches that only selfishness is rational" (quoted in Monaghan, 2003, 20). "If greed is good," Bellah concludes, "then we must also concede that we were mistaken all these years, in all the religions and philosophies of mankind, in thinking cupidity a vice instead of our chief virtue" (Bellah, 2000, 6; see also McCumber, 2011).

Consequently, none of the people who oppose the new paradigm has effectively challenged the amoral money juggernaut that took over business school education. The researchers and students learn intellectually difficult and highly abstract subjects but nothing about morality because the business schools are ill prepared to foster a normative moral outlook.

Khurana's (2007) history of business schools after 1980 confirms this judgment; it is a lament about how the business school graduates have turned into hired hands. The moral bankruptcy is exhibited in their invasion of the investor sector, not just, as Khurana says, to follow in the footsteps of the greedy, but to use their knowledge to defraud the investing public.

Heavily criticized, business schools have attempted recently to deal with the moral deficit by introducing ethics courses into their curricula. But not only the MBAs on their way to good jobs in investment firms fail to take ethics seriously; the courses themselves do not take the problem of moral order seriously.

Not unexpectedly, conservative American Christianity's acceptance of the behavioral norms and values of American managerialism cut it off from postmodernist concerns about "the notion of leadership" entailing "moral responsibility to others" and the making of "ethical choices," which are at the heart of Critical Management Education's discussion of US managerial capitalism. Instead Christian-inspired business school ethics courses concentrate on a "heroic, transactional, and transformational vision of managerialism leadership," based on "abstract, universal ethical doctrines that do not question the macroeconomic system" (Cunliffe, 2009, 91–92).

This transactional, universalist outlook permeates textbook literature. For example, Wayne Grudem in his *Business for the Glory of God* (2003) picks out transaction subjects (productivity, buying and selling, profit making, competition, and borrowing and lending) and asks managers to deal with them in a biblical way, and Michael Zigarelli in his *Managing by Proverbs* (2008) discusses the use of the teachings in the Book of Proverbs under five management transformational headings: Personal Foundations of Success; Building a Competitive Workforce; Cultivating a Culture of Connections; Evaluating and Rewarding Performance; and Controlling Workplace Conflict. The appeal to the personal morality of the managers leaves the student unaware of the importance of systemic morality – the impropriety when one element within a firm is a privileged caste that is exclusively empowered to decide moral issues.

Considering the pervasive influence of postmodernism in US academia at the end of the twentieth century, it might seem implausible for it to have had so little impact on the teaching of business ethics in US business schools – until we remember the sustained effort made in them after World War Two to turn management into an amoral science (Khurana, 2007, 195–290). Aside from the occasional isolated course on business ethics, students are exposed to secularized systems of impersonal management decision-making. They are taught that decisions are to be made according to how they affect the bottom line; they learn to evaluate employees in terms of how their performance affects profitability. Numbers matter most when figuring whether to hire and fire, to keep, reduce, or eliminate employee benefits, to outsource, to build new plants abroad or close old ones. And a de-moralized management caste exclusively makes the decisions. Some moral order!

CHAPTER 3

Managerialism and the decline of the US automobile industry

In this chapter we move from a macro to a micro dimension in order to demonstrate specifically the serious handicap that managerialism imposed on US industry. The historian must be careful to delineate what is being discussed when approaching the topic. There are many reasons for industries to grow or decline that are not directly related to management systems. Events can turn on strategic decision making (over products for example), or on government fiscal, educational, and taxation policies, or on macroeconomic developments, or on war and revolution, climate change, resource depletion, or many other matters that were/are constantly evoked to explain US industrial decline in the old staple manufacturing industries after 1975.

Then, a comparison of management systems might reveal very little about US manufacturing failure, especially when evaluating the success of foreign transplants in their competition with American firms, which is one focus here. The first significant transplants to America from Japan happened in the television industry with the establishment of assembly factories in the 1970s. By 1998, "Japanese companies owned all television assembly factories operating in the United States" (Kenney, 1999, 257). Successful Japanese automobile transplants arrived later, and theirs is a different management story from that of electronics firms.

Martin Kenney, in a study that compares Japanese television assembly transplants to Japanese automobile transplants, points out that for technical reasons

> automobile manufacturing spent less on R&D than consumer electronics, had lower engineer-to-operator ratios, had lower automation, [and] used many more parts in assembly (30,000 to 40,000 compared to less than 2,000) in much longer assembly lines (one kilometer compared to 100 meters). Assembly time in an automobile factory per unit varied from 10–20 hours compared to 27 minutes in a television assembly plant. The role of operators was much greater in automobile assembly than in television production; automobile manufacturing required more on-the-job training and more interactive work. Automobile production technology needed employees with more inter-relational skills. (Kenney, 1999, 273)

To achieve results, Japanese automobile transplants had to bring more of the Japanese Manufacturing System (JMS) from home than Japanese transplants in consumer electronics – and they did. The electronics firms copied US management methods in television transplant factories, instead of, as in Japanese automobile transplants, importing theirs.

The automobile industry is treated here because it fits our thesis that the amoral management caste running US mass production facilities in the late twentieth century lost out in global competition to better-run foreign producers with high employee-dependent forms of management and a strong collaboration ethic. The topic selection, however, is not just convenient. Detroit's Big Three (Ford, Chrysler, and General

Motors) might be a shadow of their former selves today, and somewhat insignificant in the current American industrial park. However, the automobile industry in world manufacturing has not diminished in importance; rather, automobile manufacturing (like other manufacturing industries) shifted to foreign firms, headquartered primarily in Germany and Japan.

In Germany, despite the sluggishness of domestic manufacturing generally between 1994 and 2004, when German industry as a whole shed 13 percent of its jobs, employment in German automobile firms at home augmented 21 percent. German firms created 135,000 new jobs domestically, paid €36 billion in wages and salaries annually, and earned annual export surpluses of €80 billion, while re-investing annually €12 billion in research and development (one third of German industrial R&D investment).

In 2003, indirectly upstream and downstream in the German economy, 5.3 million German jobs (one of every seven people employed) depended on automobiles. This amounted to a splendid intrapreneurial achievement at a time when people criticized Germans for their lack of entrepreneurism (Locke and Schöne, 2004). At the new millennium, German automobile makers had fashioned a worldwide network of 2,000 production plants. In the ten years 1995–2005 the firms doubled their revenues, with 75 percent of sales in 2005 outside Germany as opposed to 50 percent ten years before. Production of German vehicles reached 20 percent of world output in 2005, with production abroad growing the fastest (a total of 5,469,114 units). The Japanese story is even more impressive. As the century turned, Japanese firms manufactured more automobiles than any other country, and they produced them throughout the world (Table 3.1).

Table 3.1

Units of production – Japanese automobile firms, 2005–2006

Asia	4,174,624
Europe (EU + non-EU)	1,603,506
Europe (EU only)	1,420,391
North America (including US) – 1 out of 6 being produced in Canada	4,092,493
US alone	3,386,751

Source: *News from the Japanese Automobile Manufacturing Association (JAMA)*, Issue 4, 2006.

One way for companies to globalize is through acquisitions. American and European carmakers followed that strategy. Thus, Ford acquired Jaguar, Volvo, and Mazda, General Motors took over Opel, Daimler-Benz amalgamated with Chrysler, and Renault bought heavily into Nissan Motors. Major Japanese firms decided in the main to develop overseas manufacturing primarily on greenfield sites. Honda opened the first transplant in the US in 1979; other Japanese firms followed suit in the early 1980s. In 1986 these firms produced 617,000 units in North America, 12 percent of Japanese car sales in the US (3.4 million Japanese cars sold). Twenty years later (2006), 63 percent of the cars Japanese companies sold in the US were assembled there, many more than the 2,300,000 vehicles Japanese firms exported from home into the expanding US market. In 2005 Japanese transplants in North America made 4.09 million vehicles. In two decades Japanese automobile manufacturers in the US invested $28 billion in a dozen assembly plants and thirteen parts plants (Table 3.2).

Table 3.2

Japanese auto parts manufacturers in North America

	1979	1980–4	1985–9	1990–4	1995–8	Total
USA	5	6	64	21	17	113
Canada			7	1	3	11
Mexico	1		2	5	3	11
Totals	6	6	73	27	23	135

Source: T. Rutherford, P. Parker, and T. Koshiba, "Global, Local or Hybrid? Evidence of Adaptation among Japanese Automobile Plants in Japan, the United States and Canada." *Environment* 29(3) (2001), 19.

Twenty years of sustained effort resulted in the remarkable presence of Japanese firms in global automobile manufacturing. For some firms, overseas production eventually exceeded that in Japan. Honda, for example (2002), made 778,000 units in Japan, 1,220,000 in North America and 178,000 in Europe. Because of the high stakes, there is nothing trivial about studying the effects of managerialism on America's automobile industry. The indictment against managerialism in this industry is serious.

Managerialism in US automobile manufacturing

The issue is the mass production of automobiles. In the US, the pace setter, Henry Ford, erected a showcase plant in the early 1920s at the River Rouge to minimize waste and maximize output and profits through a closely coordinated production system. "Ford's River Rouge plant," in H. Thomas Johnson's words,

> worked like clockwork to make a standardized product. Ford spoke proudly of turning iron ore, silica, and latex into finished vehicles in less than three and a half days, at the lowest cost in the world ...The lead times and costs achieved in his River

Rouge plant had never been equaled before – nor have they been equaled since. (Johnson, 1992, 37)

After World War Two, customers wanted much greater product variety than Ford's River Rouge plant had been originally designed to produce. Indeed, until the late 1920s the River Rouge plant produced only the legendary Model-T "in any color the customer wants, so long as it's black." Postwar, in order to cope with the market demand for a variety of vehicle types and to make them in one plant, American engineers and production managers "decoupled the line," which allowed different processes to operate at independent rates, and they created inventory buffers to handle the imbalances appearing between the decoupled processes. "Henry Ford did not require inventory buffers at the River Rouge in the early 1920s. Most American manufacturing plants could not operate without such buffers by the end of the 1950s" (Johnson, 1992, 38). Figure 3.1 portrays mass production in varieties with decoupled parts fabrication in batches and inventory preceding final assembly. Varieties of components and parts are produced in batches and then warehoused until needed in final assembly to make finished vehicles to be sent on to the dealers.

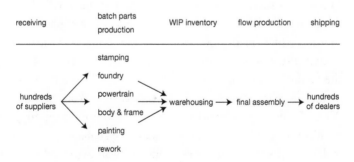

Figure 3.1
Big Three mass production process – post World War Two

The decoupling of myriad operations that had been linked in a contiguous flow at Ford's River Rouge plant forced American management to create information systems charged with planning, production programming, factory forecasting, financial reporting, standard cost budgeting, production target setting, and overall coordination of the decoupled production process. They were designed and run by managers from outside the production process, who interfered in it to control results.

Cost of equipment that sustained information management flows in Big Three manufactories (mainframe computers and supplies) and other overhead costs mushroomed in a Decoupled Batch-and-Assembly Manufacturing Plant. Management paid for these overheads by exploiting the system of quantitative control-and-reporting measures it had devised. By speeding up throughput in each detached production segment, managers thought they could obtain huge savings from mass production. Although total costs driven up by rising overheads increased, the "savings" ostensibly would come through reduced cost per unit of output as output volume rose faster than total cost.

Since the money men at corporate headquarters were interested in profits, the management system provided for top-down control and bottom-up financial reporting. General Motors's financial committee already in the 1920s relied for investment decisions on a rate-of-return analysis of predicted returns, which made moneymaking the "guiding vision or overall direction for further development of the business or the factory" (Rother, 2010, 62). "We are not in the business of making cars, we are in the business of making money," Alfred P. Sloan, Jr., President of General Motors, 1923–1937, proclaimed; GM management installed systems of decision making in the divisions for reporting to headquarters "based heavily on analysis of reported managerial accounting data" (Rother, 2010, 63).

The Japanese production system

There was nothing particularly Japanese about either the strategy or the methods Japanese automobile manufacturers used in their rise to prominence after World War Two (Tsutsui, 1998). Eiji Toyoda's statement to the head of Ford Motor Company (Philip Caldwell) in 1982 that Toyota had learned its famous lean production system from observing contiguous, linked, low-inventory production in Henry Ford's River Rouge factory was perfectly true.

To mount successful automobile export industries, the Japanese, like their American competitors, needed to figure out how to couple variety with low-cost volume production. They solved the problem differently from Detroit. Since accumulating inventory in upstream batch production of components and parts increased costs, Taiichi Ohno at Toyota improved on Ford's system by extending the contiguous flow found in his final assembly to all upstream component- and parts-making operations so as to slash the cost of producing variety to customer demand. In particular, this meant reducing the time it took to make necessary changeovers needed for different products. Longer changeover times meant more line downtime, reduced volume and increased costs.

The use of engineers on the factory floor, Professor Yamashine observed (Yamashine, 1991), resulted in the remarkable superiority that Japanese firms achieved in "average setup time," as in the die changes needed to achieve manufacturing variety. Greater speed in changing dies allowed the Japanese firm to have more frequent setups, thereby permitting much greater manufacturing flexibility. Because Japanese engineers not only developed and designed products, but also went to the shop floor and worked with line employees to solve problems, they gained first-hand knowledge of the manufacturing process and obtained the quick feedback necessary for close and continuous study of the relationship between machine design and the die-change process. This allowed the Japanese production people to keep costly downtimes to a minimum and permitted them to pursue continuous improvement, fine-tuning, and product variety.

Just as Toyota learned production flows from the River Rouge plant, so did Japanese engineers borrow the quality control techniques used in manufacturing from American experts. Walter Shewhart developed statistical process control (SPC) in the 1930s at Bell Laboratories, and then, assisted by W. Edwards Deming, applied the methods to war production. Kaoru Ishikawa, who helped transfer quality control methods to Japanese industry, maintains that SPC helped the United States win the war. Eager to improve manufacturing processes, the Japanese Union of Scientists and Engineers, founded in 1949, began to invite American quality control experts to Japan. W. Edwards Deming visited in 1951 and returned to Japan frequently thereafter; Joseph Juran went over in 1955, and Armand V. Feigenbaum in 1960. They helped introduce quality control ideas into Japanese industry.

Japanese experts made contributions of their own. Shigeo Shingo, a mechanical engineer at Toyota and Mitsubishi shipbuilding, as well as Kaoru Ishikawa, professor at the University of Tokyo, and Genichi Taguchi, a statistician, improved SPC for shopfloor employees (Ishikawa,1985, 14). Shingo promoted the "zero defects," or *poka yoke* objective, advancing worker-based total management control systems; Ishikawa simplified SPC theory, creating the fishbone cause–effect diagram "used in process analysis as part of the continuous improvement system." Taguchi formulated the Quadratic Loss Function, which measured the multiplier effect of minute quality losses along the process line. Because of the efforts of statistical and industrial specialists, Japanese automobile manufacturers transformed the primarily technical SPC methods, imported from America, into highly efficient shopfloor process control management systems. As Japanese manufacturers learned to fine-tune process, comparative excellence developed steadily over the years. At Toyota, quality had become an integral part of management by 1954 as did the soon-to-become-famous quality control circles in 1962. Mark Fruin and Toshihiro Nishiguichi claim that the Toyota production system evolved through three stages (Fruin and Nishiguichi, 1993). Immediately postwar it operated like the American Taylorist managerial model (flows of information and structures and processes top-down, with managerial prerogatives exclusively in the hands of Toyota's managers). Then in the early 1960s a network production model emerged that turned into an employee-empowered learning model during the two decades after 1970. H. Thomas Johnson studied the more mature system at Toyota.

There is no need to describe the famous techniques that Toyota steadily incorporated into its production line to cut material-and-time waste in a continuous flow production that included product variety. Suffice it simply to name some of them found today at the Georgetown facility in Kentucky: Takt time production (production paced to the rate of customer demand, so many seconds allotted per vehicle before the line moves), standardized work, *Jidoka* (the Andon stop cord), Just In Time (JIT) delivery from suppliers inside and outside the factory (only the necessary product, at the necessary time, in the necessary quantities), *Heijunka* (level sequencing of production), Total Quality Control, and *Kanban.*

Johnson named the Toyota Production System "Management by Means," whereby management concentrates not on mindlessly driving work to achieve the desired financial results (as in the Big Three) but on perfecting the means of production through collaboration. (If the means are in order, the results are as excellent as one can expect, until people improve the means a step further.) He called the production system in the Big Three firms "Management by Results." Mike Rother contrasted the thinking behind the two managements as follows: "Financial targets and results are vital, of course, but for long-term organization survival the question How do we achieve those financial results should often be preceded by the question What do we need to do with our processes, products, or services to meet customer needs?" (Rother, 2010, 126). Johnson juxtaposed a list of phrases that contrasted the behavioral traits suited to Big Three management-driven "decoupled" manufacturing with those of the Toyota collaborative-continuous-process production system (see Table 3.3).

Table 3.3
Production behavioral values – Big Three and the
Toyota Production System

Big Three	TPS
The "I" stands alone	Relationships are reality
Control the result	Nurture relationships
Follow finance-driven rules	Master life-oriented practices
Manipulate output to control costs	Provide output as needed on time
Increase speed of work	Change how work is done
Specialize and decouple processes	Enhance continuous flow
An individual is the cause: blame	Mutual interaction is the cause: reflect

Source: H. T. Johnson and A. Bröms, *Profits Beyond Measure: Extraordinary Results through Attention to Work and People*. New York: Free Press, 2000, 186–87.

TPS process-oriented behavior is not management in the Chandlerian sense, and those raised and educated after World War Two in the US have had difficulty comprehending it. Johnson, observing this difficulty, trenchantly remarked in 2010: "Western observers [have] mistakenly attribute[d] Toyota's success to a set of practices they (Westerners) labeled 'lean' in the 1980s." These practices can be learned by US managers, but they have difficulty, with their management mindset, grasping what is "…more basic in Toyota than those specific countermeasures. The company's distinctive way of thinking … drives it constantly to strive for an ideal state, sometimes referred to as 'True North.' This problem-solving process," Johnson continued, "and the underlying thinking is described fully for the first time in English in *Toyota Kata*, a new book (2010) by Mike Rother" (Johnson, 2010, 3).

In his book, Rother made similar distinctions:

> Toyota's way, as it is sometimes called, is characterized less by its tools or principles than by sets of procedural sequences – thinking and behavior patterns – that when repeated over and over in daily work lead to the desired outcome. These patterns are the context within which Toyota's tools and principles are developed and function. (Rother, 2010, 15)

For managers in the US, to concentrate on tools and principles is to miss the point.

Rother describes a *kata* as "a routine or method that is practiced and used time and again … until it becomes second nature" (Rother, 2010, 15). Toyota has two *katas*; one is designed to instill patterns of thinking and behavior in its employees that bring about continuous improvement in work processes and products; the second is a coaching *kata* that teaches people the improvement *kata*.

The primary job of Toyota's managers and leaders is not with improvement per se, but with increasing the improvement capability of people, which is achieved through a mentor–mentee relationship (and all people in Toyota have one), based on respect and obligation. In US automobile manufacturing, routinely the cultivation of employees' improvement skills was left to human resource managers in the training and development departments of firms. Training devolved to classroom teaching and simulation exercises; at Toyota, to insure that the improvement *kata* is internalized, "managers and leaders teach the improvement *kata* by guiding the people in making real improvement in real processes. It is not something management does that is separated from the work process" (Rother, 2010, 218). The mentors, moreover, do not try to bring solutions to problems. What management brings to the organization is a *kata* for how people should act when faced with a situation. This is management similar to the educational philosophy and method operating in Japanese schools K–12. "Toyota's attention to process and the thinking it generated," Johnson concluded, "led to the company's many decades of remarkable financial performance." (Table 3.4)

Table 3.4
Comparative performance of major automobile firms, 2006

	Sales (million units)	Sales ($ billion)	Profits ($ billion)	Market value ($ billion)	Workforce
GM	8.3	191	– 10.9	20	335,000
Toyota	8.2	176	+ 12.5	208	285,000
Ford	6.6	153	– 12.7	16	300,000
Volkswagen	5.2	118	+ 5.2	43	344,000
Daimler/Chrysler	4.8	185	– 1.7*	65	382,000

* losses incurred at Chrysler
Source: S. Schifferes, "The Decline of Detroit." BBC News, July 1, 2007, 5.

The response of US managerialism to the Japanese automobile challenge

Ronald Dore first drew the West's attention to Japanese manufacturing in 1973; for the most part US automakers and the public greeted the challenge with disbelief. By the end of the decade, however, US automobile managers got serious. Robert Lutz, head of Ford's operations in Europe and later a vice president at GM, sent scores of his people to Japan in 1979 to study production methods. GM entered into a joint agreement with Toyota (New United Motor Manufacturing, Inc., NUMMI) in 1984 in order to introduce already acknowledgedly superior Toyota production methods into its operations at a plant in Fremont, California. Studies about Japanese lean production multiplied throughout the 1980s (700 articles were published in the US on Just In Time between 1985 and 1990), culminating in the universally touted book by J.F. Womack, D.T. Jones, and D. Roos, *The Machine That Changed the World* (1990).

By 1990, knowledgeable Americans realized that neither size, nor low wages, nor higher investment accounted for Japanese success but "a new combination of technological and organizational innovation" (Locke, 1996, 172). Smart people stopped asking whether "lean production" would triumph. As Andrew P. Graves stated, "It has become obvious ... that the built-in training mechanisms and continuous improvement of technology [Westerners] have discovered in Japan have culminated in the development of a lean production system, which has replaced Fordism as world practice in manufacturing" (Graves, 1993, 1). Study turned into sustained effort to transfer Japanese production methods to US firms.

However, the very structure and practice of US automobile governance that the management caste had set up frustrated the transfer of these practices. The adversarial stance between management and blue-collar workers characteristic of American industrial relations, which is at the heart of managerialism, encouraged workforce resistance to the implementation of job rotation, multiple skilling, and group work, practices that were necessary to a well-functioning work process modeled on Japanese practice. US unions fought hard to protect workers' interests written in collective bargaining agreements (Pil and MacDuffie, 1999, 43). Nor did American employers and employees readily accept the elimination of status distinctions between blue- and white-collar workers, which disappeared in Japan after World War Two, and whose absence is considered to be essential to an improvement *kata*, the essence of which is solidarity and common purpose.

The US management caste, however, most resisted the adoption of a Japanese-style improvement *kata*. Many of the agency, property rights, and transaction costs models used in Big Three governance could not easily be reconciled with Japanese production systems in which management and unions are not determined adversaries, and asymmetries between managers and employees in terms of voice, rights, and benefits are significantly muted (Liker, Fruin, and Adler, 1999, 10). Toyota's JIT production methods were "dramatically opposed to the economic order and guiding principles of American manufacturing and to US plant reliance on technologies such as Material Requirements Planning II [MRPII] for shop floor scheduling" (Liker, Fruin, and Adler, 1999, 10).

In America "only engineering experts could develop scientifically accurate work methods" (Liker, Fruin, and Adler, 1999, 10). In America job design and quality control were traditionally the tasks of management. Quality control managers had operators forward information on process abnormalities, which they would put in Pareto charts in order to identify the most important process abnormalities to deal with. But, as Mike

Rother observed, "The information provided by Pareto charts usually comes too late to be useful for the process improvement efforts" that Toyota's *kata* required (Rother, 2010, 181). In Japanese automobile manufacturing in general and in Toyota in particular, engineers always work closely with line workers in the production process, and in matters of process abnormalities first-line managers work with operators to solve them immediately on the line. Japanese supervisors and team leaders know all the jobs in their jurisdictions in detail and are generally selected as supervisors because they were/are the best operators.

On the other hand, in Big Three Detroit firms, middle management's will to effect change not only was "lukewarm" but the capacity to do so was lacking. American managers had little shopfloor experience and, accordingly, did not contribute much to shopfloor efficiency through hands-on work with line employees. Management, separated from the workforce in US automobile firms, customarily used, and workers heard, a language of command. By contrast the TPS's improvement *kata* required group-oriented consensus making, the cultivation of relational skills, and tacit learning, of the kind Ikujiro Nonaka and Hirotake Takeuchi described in their 1995 book that US reformers read on *The Knowledge-Creating Company*.

Considering the existential nature of the threat, the response of the management caste in US automobile firms was at best inadequate. As Liker, Fruin, and Adler put it in 1999: "The American companies that adopt Japanese practice do not go quite so far and do not get quite the performance [as do Japanese transplants]. The Big Three do not put the same effort into training and socializing ... and do not reach performance levels of their Japanese competitors in Japan or North America" (28).

Eleven years later, after thirty years of the Japanese automobile challenge, with major US firms bankrupt or teetering on bankruptcy, a frustrated Mike Rother wrote: "I do sense a growing discussion in the USA that the outcome-oriented approach [of managerialism] described on pages 62–71 of *Toyota Kata* should be changed to better match the challenges we face today. I do not, however, sense this [need] coming from MBA schools. They are, it seems, thus far only at the 'bargaining' stage of change, à la If we add some ethics courses can we please keep our highly lucrative, reductionist, manage-by-results, ROI-based approach?" (email to Robert Locke, May 2, 2010).

German automobile firms' response to the Japanese challenge

The Japanese invasion of the US market did not harm only American car companies. Volkswagen's yearly exports to the US fell by 50 percent between 1965 and 1975, down from 1 million vehicles. In the 1980s, European Economic Community (EEC) car manufacturers' share of the US market dropped from 10 to 4 percent of total sales. While Japanese exports to America cut into Europe's share of the US import market, Japanese exports to Europe menaced European home markets. Japanese import sales grew substantially in the 1980s; Volkswagen sales scarcely augmented. And European branch manufacturers of US firms (Opel and Ford) saw their niche markets shrink.

For some German "Japanization" pioneers such as Professor Horst Wildemann, the awakening started in the 1970s. In Brussels at the European Foundation for Management Development (EFMD) in 1978, a Japanese colleague, also an EFMD visiting professor, introduced him to JIT, *kanban* (continuous improvement), and other Japanese techniques. He read more deeply in the English-language literature on Japan (little was available in German, and Japanese study programs were poorly developed in German higher education). Wildemann became, with his associates, an important part of the work-process innovation story in Germany (Locke interview, July 21, 1994). His activities provide a useful reference from which to gauge Germany's response to the lean production challenge.

In 1988, he attended a special seminar at the Massachusetts Institute of Technology, sponsored by Volkswagen, at which James Womack, who was then finishing the co-authored book *The Machine That Changed the World* (1990), talked about lean production. Real innovators, Wildemann affirms, are not up on the latest publication; they know about its contents before it appears. Wildemann had already taught the new work-process methods to active managers; at Passau in 1981 he held three seminars with an attendance of about sixty. By 1983 attendance at a seminar, with managers from all over Europe, grew to 1,500. By the decade's end German management had fully awakened to the Japanese challenge to their automobile industry. Dr. Dieter Kirchner, of the Gesamt-Metall Employer Association, remarked that every German automobile manager had a German translation of *The Machine that Changed the World* on his/her desk (Locke interview, July 18, 1994). And it was dog-eared.

By the mid 1990s, Wildemann and his colleagues had implemented work-process changes in the plants of some very famous firms, including Mercedes-Benz, Grundig, Philips, and Volkswagen. At Volkswagen he spent three years teaching small-group quality control management techniques in five-day courses to over 2,500 managers.

Because of this hard work, the German automobile industry transformed itself along Japanese lean production lines. Germany's luxury car producers (BMW, Audi, Porsche, and Daimler-Benz) put themselves through lean manufacturing reform in their plants. Among the large-volume German producers, Volkswagen changed from a "multinational company with global activities" into a "global production network" (Speidel, 2002,16). The company adopted a platform strategy which relied "on a global production network with parallel productions of the same models at different sites, allowing for the shift of production of cars around the world, depending on market development and business strategies" (Speidel, 2002, 16).

There is, however, an incongruity here: why were German automobile firms able to transform themselves so successfully when the US firms stumbled? German producers undoubtedly profited from having followed a different overall strategy from the Americans. Before the crisis began, Germany concentrated on high-volume luxury car production. Although the Japanese moved up-market to challenge them with Lexus, Acura, and Infiniti automobiles, the German firms' reputation permitted them to dominate luxury car markets (Mercedes-Benz, BMW, Porsche, and Audi). But the nonluxury big-volume producer Volkswagen also emerged as the largest mass production firm in Europe and one of the largest in the world. Clearly, something in German organizational culture, unlike that of the US, permitted the German automobile firms successfully to revamp their production systems along Japanese lines (Locke, 1999; Lewis, 1985, 93).

German work culture

When dealing with the evolution of German work mentality, start with the term *Beruf*. *Beruf* means a "calling" or an occupation, and the term is frequently, as Peter Lawrence observed, combined with the word *Lern*, as *Lernberuf*, an occupation composed of a set of skills and knowledge that have to be learned if a person is to exercise the *Beruf*. In Germany, the *Lernberuf* is a holdover from the guilds (the preindustrial handicraft apprenticeship system of qualification) in the modern German factory organization; it still has a legally protected status. This transformed medieval handicraft guild tradition serves modern industry through a system of apprenticeship and semi-apprenticeship training, combined with school study, which provides a world-class manufacturing economy with a highly skilled labor force.

In German factories, the German first-line manager, the *Meister* (foreman), is a product of this system. After an apprenticeship that results, upon examination, in a certificate of qualification as a skilled worker, the aspirant to *Meister* undergoes years of on-the-job training, independent study and special examination, to obtain his or her *Meisterbrief* and with it the great respect for the holder's expertise that permeates the German workplace. This apprenticeship system ties the *Meister* to the skilled labor force under him or her.

Above the *Meister*, middle and even higher management (including the board level) is also tied into the apprenticeship system. This happens because a large number of German middle management engineers earn their diplomas in *Fachschulen* (*grad.-Ing.*, raised to the status of *Fachhochschulen* in the 1970s with the degree *Dipl.-Ing. FH*). To gain entry into *Fachschulen* (*Fachhochschulen*) students had to have completed an apprenticeship in some technical or commercial *Lernberuf,* just like the fledgling *Meister*. Then in school the practical orientation continues by combining course work with stints working in praxis.

Some managers, after A-levels (the *Abitur)*, attended university-level schools to study for the degree *Dipl.-Ing.* – a longer course of study with much more theoretical education. Even so, neither these students nor their professors were entirely cut off from the practical world. Professors in university-level engineering departments and faculties needed to have at least five years' work experience in industry to get a chair; they could, therefore, talk knowledgeably about the real work world with their students. On the other hand, students in engineering studies in the *Fachschulen*

(*Fachhochschulen*) were not completely isolated from the influence of more theoretical university studies because their teachers were drawn from university engineering graduates (*Dipl.-Ing.*). Educationally, therefore, managers in German industry who studied in *Fachschulen/Fachhochschulen* were connected to universities, with their more theoretical studies, because their teachers had university engineering degrees, and to the system of *Lernberuf* because they had had to complete an apprenticeship in order to gain entry into a *Fachschule/Fachhochschule*.

Peter Lawrence discusses these qualification interconnections in his book about West German factory managers (Lawrence, 1980). He describes the workplace as a gradient chain of capacities running from the unskilled, through the skilled, through the skilled educated in science, to the science-educated with practical experience. He describes a qualification diversity that is united by a common respect for sapiential forms of learning, which make the German workworld one wherein recognition and promotion depend more on demonstrated job performance (*Leistung*) than academic diplomas. He emphasized how much the Germans at all levels of a manufacturing organization respect *Technik* – that blending of knowledge and skill entailed in the making of quality products or the delivery of quality services on time – how they see no conflict between theory and practice because good practice requires good theory. *Fachkenntnisse* (knowhow in one's specialty) is the prime qualification in the workplace; the term is not pejorative in Germany. On the contrary, a person's expertise is respected, and that person is called upon for his or her opinion by those superior as well as inferior in the hierarchy.

Lawrence related that German companies

> exploit the practical and experiential knowledge of workers and lower supervisors in what might be thought of as decision areas which [in America] would be management's prerogative. The

most obvious example is machinery purchase; not whether to buy, but what to buy. It is standard practice for someone with practical experience of working the relevant machine types – a skilled worker, a charge hand, or foreman – to attend machinery purchase meetings, hold forth to the 'higher ups' and critically examine the technical specification sheets prepared by Engineering. It is also not uncommon for the same people to receive ... potential suppliers, or go on trips to examine machinery at trade fairs, manufacturers' premises, or *in situ* at some other firm ... When someone has to do something outside, or represent the company in some way, quite humble people, organizationally and socially, get sent as long as they are deemed to know enough about the matter in hand. (Lawrence, 1980, 137)

German hierarchies are flatter than American, supervisors' spans of control are broader, qualified people are given more responsibility and allowed to exercise it. If a problem occurs in a factory, the *Meister* tries to fix it before bringing in his supervisor, but if he does, the *Meister* is ready with a list of suggested remedies. "Production managers expand 'sideways' into staff functions and sometimes 'backwards' and 'forwards' into Design and Sales." Lawrence talks about organizational flexibility, the German tendency, unlike the Americans, not to "externalize" specialized knowledge but to incorporate specialist and technical knowledge into the line itself and "to expect production workers to do as much as possible for themselves rather than to depend on staff" (Lawrence, 1980, 137). The *Meister* does quite a lot for his supervisor, is able to do it, and is expected to do it. Such well-knit organizations learn new production processes well.

Codetermination

Codetermination also facilitated the introduction of Japanese work processes into German manufacturing. When the system began, German management, trade unions, and employee

representatives were not equals. "On the one side of the negoti-
ation table," the IG Metall trade unionist Hans Preiss observed,
"sits the employer with hundreds of semesters of university
studies, on the other, [employee-elected] works councilors ... to
defend the interest of employees with only quick cram courses
under their belts" (Preiss, 1979, 502). Since paragraphs 90 and
91 of the Works Constitution Act specified that changes in the
regulation of work conditions must be based on "solid knowledge of the sciences of work (*gesicherte arbeitswissenschaftliche
Erkenntnisse*)," poorly informed employee representatives
could not be equal partners in work process reform discussions.
Or, as another trade union spokesman commented:

> If we ask our colleagues in the [trade union] Education Center
> why thousands each year ask for seminar places, despite long
> waiting lists and increased conflict with employers about release
> time, the answer comes from the daily life of works councilors,
> shop stewards, and youth representatives. There, in the life of the
> firm, where conflict is unavoidable, they find themselves saddled
> with tasks for which they are insufficiently prepared. If works
> council business was reduced uniquely to knowledge of laws and
> regulations, more than thirty texts would have to be mastered.
> Considering that on the [employer] side most people have
> several semesters' professional study and special training, then
> the knowledge gap at the outset between the different interest-
> representatives is clear. (Johannson and Weissbach 1979, 119)

Probably the 1972 Works Constitution Act spurred efforts the
most to redress this imbalance because it granted employees
release time from work in order to learn about codetermination. The trade union establishment got involved, among them
IG Metall (the automobile workers' union), which opened
the just-mentioned education center at Sprockhövel in 1971.
The center welcomed 25,000 visitors, most from German and
foreign trade unions, but also including experts and scientists

in large numbers. Sprockhövel quickly gained recognition, even in the "employers'" press, as a "model adult education school" (Preiss, 1979, 501). In 1971, some 26,000 seminar participants (works councilors, youth representatives, and shop stewards) came to the center to attend the forty-four types of seminar (12,000 works council and youth representatives during the first two years took seminars just on labor's legal rights under codetermination). By 1977, according to an IG Metall poll, almost twice as many (43,000) sought places at the center as the facility could accommodate (25,000).

The education movement spread beyond trade unions to special nonacademic training groups such as the Wuppertal Kreis and into the expanding university system and upgraded *Fachhochschulen,* which offered courses on codetermination in faculties of business economics. Since Germany had no business schools and few MBA programs, the conflict of interest that might have erupted in US higher education about management schools offering courses to firm employees could not happen. German professors of business economics (*BWL*) could teach courses on codetermination to all comers, whether from the employee or employer side, or just students seeking a degree.

Codetermination laws legally entwined employee representatives and management in German firms, and after a two-decade educational effort homogenized behavior and knowledge. In the US, management not only excludes labor from a firm's governance but the two groups constitute distinct cultures in American life.

The organizational culture in German manufacturing firms that Lawrence described and the codetermination regime that developed made it easier to carry through the transformation of the German automobile industry. Employee representatives at Volkswagen as much as the management side understood that the Japanese challenge could bring them ruin. The IG Metall trade union and VW management worked out a Collective

Agreement to Secure Production Location and Employment in 1993 (renewed periodically thereafter), which called for a proportional decrease of workers' salaries as working hours in VW's Germany-based plants were reduced, thereby giving management greater flexibly in a global context. An Agreement on Global and Forward Sourcing gave VW works councils in Germany a "last call" option when the company received bids from suppliers outside Germany. This "last call" proviso accords VW's Germany-located plants a chance to underbid the offers of external competitors, in-company or outside. To some extent the agreement, therefore, protects German workers at VW domestic plants from unemployment, but only if they are able to compete.

Moreover, the agreement, by extending responsibility for managing costs, productivity, and innovation to works councils, really brought employee representatives into the globalization process. It amounted to a tacit alliance between VW management and works councils, not so much to defend the interests of VW's German workforce as to make the works councilors junior partners with VW management competing against other companies on world markets. In this way employees assumed a proactive comanagement mode during the spread of lean manufacturing in VW's global operations (Speidel, 2002, 16).

Professor Wildemann in four years at Volkswagen worked closely with works councils and union shop stewards on lean production implementation. VW works councilors were, as he phrased it, "very intelligent people" who fully appreciated the necessity to improve work processes but also understood that the changes would reduce jobs, worktime and pay. Wildemann's group taught the new techniques to shop stewards and management. The fact that at Volkswagen, the union, IG Metall, dominated works council and shop steward elections highlights another of Wildemann's points: IG Metall promoted

the implementation of Just In Time and other new work processes. The institutions of codetermination, therefore, sustained
Volkswagen's work process reform. Wildemann's evaluation of the contributions of works councilors and shop stewards to change at Volkswagen are uniformly positive; indeed,
these employee representatives often led rather than followed
management (Locke interview, July 19, 1994).

In Germany, codetermination was not restricted to German-
owned firms. GM (Opel) and Ford, which by German law had
to have codetermination management, relied on it in work
process reform. One manager at Opel (Rüsselsheim) observed
that because of the institutions of codetermination, Opel plants
could implement shopfloor reforms better than GM plants in
the US (Streeck, 1984, 124). Whereas managerialism hindered
adaptation in the US automobile industry, German organizational culture fostered the reformation of German automobile
production, making it at the twentieth century's end a world-
class industry.

Conclusion

People have been eager to explain the emergence of the Japanese
Manufacturing System and TPS especially, ever since they set
US-dominated mass production automobile manufacturing
on its ear. Much has been written about its origins in Japanese
culture, and hence about the inability of people outside Japan to
absorb it. The cultural factor cannot be ignored in explaining its
configurations. Others have looked for mechanical and organic
affinities. Early admirers of Ford's River Rouge plant described
it as a syncopated mechanical clock. H. Thomas Johnson, studying the Toyota system while or just after reading about "the
emerging field of living" systems, detected similarities between
what he found at Toyota and the new epistemology in organic

science (Senge, 2000, xi). Later, Johnson seems to have modified his position, for in his book with Bröms (2000), in contrast to his 1992 book *Relevance Regained*, he wrote less about Toyota as a living organic system, and more about Toyota management. Automobile factories in the US, Germany, and Japan, like successful armies, are not rationally omniscient mechanical or organic systems, but expressions of the genius, or at least great talent, of men and women who devise strategies and structures that decisively change things. The organization transformers were not the fruit of systems, even though they were responsible for setting them up. It was the other way around. For them to innovate required imagination and then the ability to actualize their visions in organizations by overcoming obstacles to change. The obstacles, however, did set limits to what they could achieve. The thinking and behavioral patterns of US managerialism hindered Detroit firms from assimilating the tools and associative principles of the new Japanese production standards; the thinking and behavioral patterns inherited in German firm governance better facilitated their adoption.

CHAPTER 4

Managerialism, business schools, and our financial crisis

In the history of finance and investment banking, the US has a glorious past. Some of it is quite recent, expressed in innovations in angel-networking and the venture capitalist activities that went on outside traditional banking and investment institutions in the start-up financing that fed the phenomenal development of the information technology (IT) revolution in Silicon Valley and other locations. One reason that young entrepreneurs with big IT ideas streamed into Silicon Valley from Asia and Europe is that the easy credit the financial innovators provided gave them access to capital for start-up firms that they could not get at home (Locke and Schöne, 2004, 16–48; Reynolds et al., 1994, 2001). Silicon Valley and Boston's Route 128 are the archetypes. The amount of venture capital invested in these two regions increased from $4.3 billion in 1986 to $13 billion in 1997 (Reynolds et al., 2001, 24). In the 1990s a relatively small number of venture-capital-financed start-ups fostered 3.3 percent of total jobs in the US and 7.4 percent of GDP. Within that group, Silicon Valley and Boston's Route 128 start-ups made the major contribution.

At the same time, utilizing new global information technology, traditional banking and investment firms on Wall Street and in affiliated financial centers fomented a revolution of their own in investment capitalism. Richard Whitley in the late 1980s described the profound changes in US academia and in the world of finance that this "transformation of business finance into financial economics" brought about (Whitley, 1986). The global nature of that development can be divined from its impact on the German investment banking establishment, which had been the most dissimilar financially to the American and British systems (Albert, 1993) but saw itself in the late twentieth century sucked into the vortex of the US–UK investment dynamic.

Traditionally, German finance operated in the "kingly merchant tradition," where a firm retained a *Hausbank*, and relations with it rested on trust, that is, customers were not customers in the American sense but clients (Bátiz-Lazo, Müller, and Locke 2008). The new information technologies churning out of America allowed investors everywhere to trade in equity markets twenty-four hours a day, and the flow of monies to increase dramatically. Taking advantage of the technology and the expanding geographical opportunities accompanying the collapse of communism, and flush with petro-dollars from Middle East investors, American and UK financial houses rooted in equity markets facilitated mergers and acquisitions, debt management, and capital acquisition. They invaded previously ignored investment markets such as Germany's to the detriment of local banks and financial institutions.

By 2004 within Germany the investment arms of the two major German commercial banks (Deutsche Bank and Dresdner Bank), transacted only 38.3 percent of the mergers and acquisitions business, 21.8 percent of the German equity market business, and 16.3 percent of the debt market business

(*The Economist,* November 1, 2004, 82). J. P Morgan, Morgan Stanley, and Goldman Sachs beat the German banks in their home territory because it was an American kind of capitalism. According to *The Economist* (March 27, 2004, 75), the position of German banks declined so badly that a German agency, the Kreditanstalt für Wiederaufbau, thought it best in order to optimize results in the privatization of Deutsche Telekom to auction off large blocks of the company's shares through foreign investment banks, rather than through the investment bank arms of Deutsche Bank, Dresdner Bank and other domestic institutions.

To survive, German banks decided to adopt the new model. They moved quickly onto the turf of Anglo-American capitalism, trading in securities and engaging in business consultancy. Also, following the UK and US banks, they marketed new products and services. These included selling loan packages, credit cards, insurance, and organizing electronic banking through automated machines, and online services. Banks acted less as *Hausbanken* for large companies and held less of their clients' stock in their portfolios. In retail banking they shifted away from the kingly merchant tradition of "trust" to one of "persuasion," to letting impersonal market mechanisms set price and determine transactions. The German banks were not very successful in warding off the penetration of Wall Street and the City of London. These were splendid years for US and UK investment banks.

In the first chapter of this book we pointed out that MBAs played a negligible role in IT financial activity in Silicon Valley because they lacked the IT product knowledge and habitat networking experience necessary to exploit start-up investment opportunities. But business school participation in the new financial economics of investor capitalism was entirely another matter. MBAs increasingly found jobs in the banks, hedge funds, and investment houses of the expanding sector. Khurana's study of Harvard Business School MBAs cites a survey of first jobs for graduating Harvard Business School students: between 1965 and 1985, students' entry into financial services and consulting "rose from 23 percent to 52 percent" of graduates (Khurana, 2007, 328–29). The same shift happened in "other elite schools, such as Wharton and the business schools at Stanford and the University of Chicago." By 2005 "among the 180 principals and managing directors in the 20 largest investment firms, 73 ... [held] an MBA from one of the six elite schools (Harvard 51, Chicago 7, Columbia 6, Stanford 5, Dartmouth's Tuck 3, and Northwestern 1)" (349).

Khurana attributes the rush into finance to student greed (because of the high salaries), to neoliberal selfishness, justified primarily by the Chicago School of economists led by Milton Friedman (economic theory), and to a general decline in social responsibility in corporation boardrooms, Congress, and the business schools (public policy). The Business Roundtable (CEOs from 200 of America's largest corporations) explicitly abandoned previously subscribed-to tenets of social responsibility. In 1981 the group's Statement on Corporate Responsibility read: "Balancing the shareholders' expectations of maximum return against other priorities is one of the fundamental problems confronting corporate management. The shareholders must receive a good return, but the legitimate interest of other constituencies (customers, employees, communities, suppliers and society at large) also must have the appropriate attention ..." In 1997 the Business Roundtable announced a policy reversal: "The notion that the board must somehow balance the interests of stockholders against the interests of other stakeholders fundamentally misconstrues the role of directors" (Mintzberg, Simons, and Basu, 2002, 69). This view echoed the hard-nosed opinion of Nobel Prize winner Milton Friedman: "The social responsibility of business is to increase its profit," which augured ill for

US management's will to resist the machinations of financial predators or consider the interests of employees.

By contrast, about the same time, in a survey of German corporate managers, 86.4 percent of the respondents "accepted the social and ethical responsibility of management" – "a very high" acceptance rate among "German business leaders" (von Werder and Grundel, 2001, 102).

What did US banks, hedge fund operators, and financial investment firms expect to get out of business school graduates for paying them such good salaries? The answer: if the MBA mathematical model builders were not of much use in a Silicon Valley entrepreneurial habitat or in managing a Japanese transplant, they were perceived to be very valuable to investor capitalists on Wall Street and in the City of London. In the field of finance, new business school theorists had posited the Efficient Market Hypothesis, which meant that there were "no ambiguities about the firm's objective function: managers should maximize the current market value of the firm" (Jensen and Smith, 1984, 6). The quantification skills being learned in elite business schools permitted the professors and their graduates to design the maximization models and to concoct the highly leveraged financial packages investment firms sold to customers worldwide. In the investor sector, if not elsewhere, theory joined practice in the last quarter of the twentieth century, just as the architects of the "New Look" in business schools had predicted they would conjoin when carrying through their curricula reforms after World War Two.

The recent collapse of the investor capitalists' house of cards revealed to an unsuspecting public the darker side of the relationship that the US management caste and US business schools had cemented with finance capitalism. This darker side – dark because it has so disrupted the balance in people's lives – is the subject of this chapter.

The discussion follows two lines. First, it examines the management caste's relations with financial agents in deal making (mergers and acquisitions, leveraged private equity buyouts, etc.) that transgressed the interests of the employees and sometimes even the interests of the stockholders of the firms they managed. To gain perspective, comparisons are made with management systems in Germany and Japan – concentrating on finance. Second, we return to the theme evoked throughout the book: business school education. This time the focus is on the role elite business schools played in the development of derivatives markets.

In his testimony before the US Senate on Reforming Financial Market Regulation during the financial collapse (October 29, 2009), former hedge fund manager Robert A. Johnson noted that at that moment Wall Street was at the apex of the economy "not unlike the automotive companies [were] forty years ago." He highlighted the importance of derivatives trading to world finance:

> According to the International Swaps and Derivatives Association survey, the outstanding notional amount of derivatives is over 454 trillion dollars at mid-year 2009. The Bank for International Settlements put the number at nearly $800 trillion worldwide. Using the ISDA data, that is over 30 times US GDP. … Derivatives are not a minor dimension of US or international capital markets. They occupy a dominant position. The location of derivative exposures is also important. According to the US Office of the Comptroller of the Currency's report for June 30th 2009, US bank-holding companies with $13 trillion in assets hold a notional $291 trillion in total derivatives. Most importantly, the institutions that were at the core of the crisis and controversial bailouts in the fall of 2008 are at the same time the dominant institutions in the OTC derivatives market. In fact, according to the Office of the Comptroller of the Currency the top five institutions in terms of derivatives

exposure, Citigroup, J.P. Morgan/Chase, Bank of America, Morgan Stanley and Goldman Sachs, hold over 95 percent of derivative exposure of the top 25 Bank Holding Companies, of which 90 percent is OTC. (Johnson, 2009)

Just as the management caste's role in the decline of the US automobile industry assumes significance because of that industry's importance in the world economy, the part US business school education performed in creating derivatives markets warrants treatment because of the importance of these instruments in US and world securities trading, and because, after spectacular success in this industry initially (much like the US mass production automobile industry under managerialism), they spectacularly failed in recent years. The question posed is: to what extent can these outcomes be attributed to business school education?

Agency conflict versus managerialism

When managers fail to look after the interest of the stockholders who engaged them, finance professors call that "agency conflict." Lawrence E. Mitchell raised that subject in his book about *The Speculation Economy*. Between the 1920s and the 1970s when the management caste established itself in corporate America, the ratio between highest- and lowest-paid people in US firms widened into what has become the American norm (Mitchell, 2007, 271–74). (By 1993 the ratio between the highest- and lowest-paid in US firms was 110–160 to 1, in Japanese firms 17–18 to 1, and in German firms 23–24 to 1.) But highly paid management is not necessarily a historical example of agency conflict if US executives look after company stockholders by providing good long-term return on their investments. Mitchell claims they did just that until 1980, after which falling dividends provoked sustained stockholder complaints about management's neglect of their interests – a case of agency conflict.

This conflict arose after 1980 because the management caste increasingly lived under the tyranny of stock market valuations and the demands of institutional investors. To satisfy the latter's preoccupation with the price of a company's stock, corporate management tended to the bottom line, that is, it shored up short-term profits so that stock market analysts' expectations would be met and its company's stock price would benefit accordingly. Management policies that kept their company's stock price high diminished agency conflict between management and these institutional stockholders. If, however, the high stock valuations were achieved at the firm's expense, conflict between professional management and the firm as an entity exists, even though there is little conflict between management and its institutional stockholders. Mitchell claims that is exactly what is happening in today's speculation economy. He writes:

> A recent survey of more than four hundred chief financial officers of major American corporations revealed that almost eighty percent of them would have at least moderately mutilated their businesses in order to meet analysts' quarterly profit estimates. Cutting the budgets for research and development, advertising and maintenance and delaying hiring and new projects are some of the long-term harms they would readily inflict on their corporations. Why? Because in modern American corporate capitalism the failure to meet quarterly numbers almost always guarantees a punishing hit to the corporation's stock price. The stock price drop might cut executive compensation based on stock options, attract lawsuits, bring out angry institutional investors waving anti-management shareholder proposals and threaten executive job security if it happened often enough. Indeed, the 2006 turnover rate of 118 percent on the New York Stock Exchange alone justifies their fears. (Mitchell, 2007, 1)

This means that the management caste is willing consistently to run the corporation in the interest of stock market speculators and institutional investors in order to avoid agency conflict, while neglecting investments important to the firm's future, thereby creating a conflict between the management caste and those interested in the firm's sustainability.

The point is that judgments about the management caste's behavior depend on the metric being used. If the metric is stockholder return on investment or stock price, then the term "agency conflict" is employed, because that is the orientation professors in US business schools adopt in their treatment of the subject. "Agency conflict" is their nomenclature, but it is wedded to a proprietary conception of the firm. If the metric were based on an entity conception of the firm, on its welfare and sustainability, then the term "agency conflict" has to be discarded. That is why we substitute the term "managerialism" for "agency conflict" in this discussion. Even though there may be no agency conflict (stock prices are rising), the management caste's behavior could be compromising company sustainability and with it the livelihood of people connected with it.

A key issue, then, is the kind of metric used. In discussing the automobile industry H. Thomas Johnson and Mike Rother refer to the distinction Johnson makes between Management by Means (Toyota) and Management by Results (the Big Three). These are different metrics. Toyota is interested in making quality cars efficiently, the Big Three in making money. And the different metrics determine the production management systems and the sustainability of the companies. Just as in the automobile industry, the type of metrics involved is at the heart of this evaluation of the relationship between managerialism and finance. In any useful evaluation the question should always be raised: compared to what? That is why in this chapter once more comparisons are made with Japan and Germany, where ownership and firm governance relate differently to the finance sector than they do in US firms.

Germany and Japan

"Japanese companies," James Abegglen and George Stalk, Jr. wrote in 1988,

> differ significantly from the Western pattern. The essence of the Japanese company is the people who compose it. It does not, as the American firm, belong to the stockholders and the managers they employ to control it, but it is under the control of the people who work in it, who pay limited attention to stockholders' wishes. The company personnel, including directors who are themselves life-time employees and executives of the company, are very much part of the company. (Abegglen and Stalk, 1988, 184; see also Streeck and Yamamura, 2001)

Large German firms under regimes of codetermination (*Mitbestimmung*) differ from US corporations too. The German firm operates with a two-tier board system, supervisory board and managing board (*Aufsichtsrat* and *Vorstand*), with employee representatives holding one third to half of the seats on supervisory boards, representatives of stockholders the remainder. Employee representatives on a supervisory board have a voice in management, since a supervisory board appoints the managing board, sets its salary, and must approve important corporate policy matters like mergers and acquisitions. In addition, works constitution acts require management at the plant and company level to inform employee-elected works councils about management decisions, to consult them on a number of matters pertaining to the running of the firm, and comanage with them in specified areas such as training for the implementation of new work processes.

German and Japanese firms, moreover, relate to their outside financial environments differently from US corporations. In US firms, institutional investors are preoccupied with financial gain from share price appreciation and/or dividends. On the other hand, a Japanese firm's stock is often owned by other firms in their business groups (*kereitsu*) for strategic reasons, namely to promote "inter-firm cooperation" and to generate "business relations" (Jackson and Moerke, 2005, 351). The issue for them is not stock price, since the stock they hold in other firms is not sold, but keeping the stock in their portfolios in order to solidify profitable business contacts.

Japanese main banks act as delegated monitors by holding direct equity stakes in firms, by acting as house banks in matters of loans, and by dispatching directors to supervise firm activities, especially in difficult times (Sheard, 1994). German universal banks have been linked traditionally to business firms as *Hausbanken*, providing their clients loans, holding equity in them, and participating, through representation on the client firm's supervisory board, in their governance (Edwards and Fischer, 1994).

The US management caste has always disliked German and Japanese governance and ownership systems. That is why they vigorously opposed the passage of codetermination laws in Germany and tried to forbid group associations in Japan during the occupation. Neoliberal market-driven capitalism since 1989 has also aggressively pushed to globalize its system with the use of its stock market pricing metrics. The aggressiveness translated into a vigorous expansion of stock markets throughout the emerging economies (Shanghai, Bombay, Seoul, Taipei, Sydney, Singapore, etc.) in the 1990s to fill out a world network reporting twenty-four hours a day to the new international investor class, coupled with the propagation of managerialist outlooks in governments "inherent in the internationalization of markets" (Imasato, Martins and Pieranti, 2010). Scholars in the 1990s talked much about how the Japanese and German systems were beginning to converge on the US-UK neoliberal financial model. In Japan, the number of foreigners buying stocks listed on the Tokyo Stock Exchange jumped from 4 percent in 1990 to 18.3 percent in 2002. In Germany, banks likewise began to shed their *Hausbank* functions: whereas in 1974 senior executives from German commercial banks occupied over 20 percent of the supervisory board seats in the 100 largest German companies, in 1993 this percentage had dropped to 6.3 percent (Lütz, 2000, 1).

Anticipating this campaign's continued success, two American management experts in 2001 proclaimed that in the late twentieth century corporations lived in an era of "Discontinuity" (Foster and Kaplan, 2001). They observed that when Forbes's list of the 100 largest US corporations in 1987 is compared to Forbes's first list in 1917, only eighteen of the original 100 firms are still on the list sixty years later; sixty-one of the firms on the 1917 list no longer even exist. Scanning the S&P 500 over the period 1957–1998, they estimated that the pace of turnover at the top was accelerating so rapidly that by 2010 the average life span of an S&P-listed firm would be ten years, and that by 2020, "no more than one third of today's major corporations" on the S&P list "will have survived in an economically important way" (Foster and Kaplan, 2001, Chapter 1). This extraordinary volatility the authors attributed to the ability of market mechanisms to efficiently cull out underperforming firms (using their metrics) from the international corporate pool.

Notwithstanding the recent increase in foreign ownership of stock, in Japan the "overall amount of Foreign Direct Investment (FDI) relative to GDP has remained extremely low" (Jackson and Moerke, 2005, 351). Only 1 percent of Japanese firms, moreover, took advantage of the reform of the Commercial Code in

2002 that permitted Japanese companies to run firm governance along American lines (Vogel, 2006, 1). And the frequent neoliberal complaint that the Japanese system performed poorly in the 1990s is true only if one employs neoliberal reasoning (Locke, 2005). The touting of neoliberal market capitalism, moreover, lessened after the dot.com fiasco (2000–2001), the Enron debacle (2002), and, especially, the general crisis of finance capitalism starting in 2007 in the real estate market and then extending in 2008 to derivatives trading.

In Germany, articles about convergence on the American governance model (stressing shareholder value as opposed to employee interests) tapered off too in the last half of the first decade of the twenty-first century. They have been replaced with studies about the remodeling of German and Japanese capitalism within the context of globalization but without reference to convergence with the neoliberal market system of finance and firm governance (Lane, 2004; Dore, 2006; Hall and Thelen, 2009; Vogel, 2006; Hatoyama, 2009). There has also been trenchant criticism of the spread of global managerialism in government, which downgrades democratic participation (Imasato, Martins and Pieranti, 2010).

Through the years of aggressive neoliberalism, economists and finance experts constantly stated their case in the metrics of proprietary capital: return-on-investment to stockholders and stock valuations. But the metrics for people concerned about the firm as an entity are different. They are customer satisfaction, design and delivery of services, employee training, certifications, cooperation, relationships, reputations – all factors that contribute to the firm's sustainability (Tore Audun, email, August 12, 2010). The most important metric for people preoccupied with the firm as an entity is sustainability itself, the very opposite of the "Discontinuity" metric on which Foster and Kaplan based their analysis.

If a sustainability yardstick is used to evaluate the German and Japanese corporations, their performance is remarkable. Among the *Fortune* magazine Global 500 corporations in 2007 (July 23 issue), 139 US firms are listed and 108 German and Japanese firms. Among the thirty-seven German firms on the list, at least twenty-two had been successful firms in the nineteenth century; ten originated in the interwar period; and most of the others participated in the remarkable German economic recovery of the 1950s, the *Wirtschaftswunder* (see Table 4.1).

Table 4.1
German firms on the 2007 *Fortune* World 500 list

19th-century origins (22)	Daimler, Siemens, Deutsche Bank, DZ Bank, Deutsche Post, BASF, TUI, Landesbank Baden-Württemberg, Bayerische Landesbank, Bertelsmann, Allianz, Thyssen Krupp, Robert Bosch, Bayer, Deutsche Bahn, Franz Haniel, MAN, Henkel, Linde Group, Continental, Munich RE Group, Heraeus Holding
Interwar period (10)	Commerzbank, Lufthansa, Edeka Zentrale, Hochtief, VW, Deutsche Telekom, Alcandor, BMW, Otto Group, RWE
Post WWII (5)	E.ON, Metro, RAG, KfW Bankengruppe, Energie Baden-Württemberg

Source: *Fortune*, July 23, 2007

Table 4.2 presents nearly half (34) of the 71 Japanese firms listed in the 2007 *Fortune* Global 500 (the table excludes the local power utilities, insurance firms, and other service companies on the list; these latter constitute just less than half of the Japanese firms on the list and are located in the bottom half of the Japanese firms ranked). The firms listed in Table 4.2

together constitute the bulk of the iconic Japanese industrial and manufacturing companies that turned the country into a major manufacturing powerhouse after World War Two – and they remain, as the list shows, among the top firms decades after their rise to prominence. Here there has been "continuity" not "discontinuity."

Table 4.2
Japanese firms on the 2007 *Fortune* World 500 list

Toyota	Mitsubishi Electric	Japanese Air
Matsushita Electric	Suzuki Motors	Kobe Steel
Mitsui	Bridgestone	Hitachi
Mizuho Financial	Sanyo Electric	Mitsubishi DFJ
Mazda Motors	Nomura Holdings	Canon
Mitsubishi Heavy Ind.	Sumitomo Chemicals	JFE Holdings
Sumitomo Electric	Nissan	Sumitomo
Ricoh	Toshiba	Mitsubishi Chemicals
Toyota Industries	Nippon Steel	Mitsubishi Motors
Honda	Nippon Mining	Komatsu
Sony	Sharp	
NEC	Fuji-Film	

Source: *Fortune*, July 23, 2007

Their very sustainability and that of large German firms as well (e.g., in automobile and machines tools) helps explain the volatility in the rankings of US firms. Competition with the foreign firms, not the mechanism of stock markets, diminished the US firms, sent them into bankruptcy, or made them easy pickings for promoters of mergers and acquisitions. Firms in many US industrial sectors suffered. In the tire industry, United States Rubber and Royal went under, and rising Bridgestone bought declining Firestone; in the steel industry once-mighty US Steel fell to 479th on the 2007 *Fortune* Global 500 list; previously renowned US manufacturers of machine tools (e.g. Burgmaster) and manufacturers of electronic products (Philco, Zenith, RCA, etc.) were replaced by Sony, Matsushita, Sanyo, and others; and Japanese automobile manufacturers crowded out or replaced American firms at the top of the 500. If a sustainability metric is used, then Japanese and German large corporations perform much better than American ones.

Volatility on the US lists also increased because of the appearance of new icon firms, most of them emerging from the IT revolution (Hewlett-Packard, Oracle, Intel, Microsoft, Dell, Google, Apple, etc.). Observing the presence of the new IT firms, and their absence among German and Japanese corporations on the lists, most Americans attribute their superior performance in the new industries to the greater entrepreneurial spirit of American free market capitalism. Although it is difficult to investigate why Japanese and German new high technology firms did not do better, it is possible to investigate why and how the Americans did so well. The US advantage in IT definitely did not stem from free market capitalism.

Rather, government-sponsored research produced a highly sophisticated core of scientists and engineers who subsequently turned to commercial activity. Not just products and ideas but the brains needed to continue the development process came out of government-sponsored research. The "huge buildup of US military R&D in the 1950s and 1960s provided a larger stock of scientists and engineers than in any other Western country" (Alic et al., 1992, 114). By 1963 the percentage of the US workforce consisting of graduate scientists and engineers was at least three times that of its principal industrial rivals in the free world.

Much evidence supports the claim that the presence of a large group of scientists and engineers working on government projects subsequently developed market-oriented IT firms. Joshua Lerner's survey in the 1980s provides useful numbers. It shows that 24.2 percent of scientists and engineers with defense-related positions in 1982 had shifted to civilian jobs four years later, but it also shows that 26.5 per cent of the scientists and engineers that had been in defense-oriented jobs in 1986 had been in non-defense positions four years earlier (Alic et al., 1992, 118). A dynamic interrelationship existed between the two groups.

There is anecdotal evidence too. Xerox's research unit at Palo Alto (PARC), which developed the technology that Steve Jobs copied for Apple's Macintosh project, hired "hundreds of ARPA superstars from government laboratories after 1970" (Rheingold, 1991, 85). Both Germany and Japan were forbidden by their former enemies and new friends to work on atomic, radar, and computer research after the war until the late 1950s. Neither country built up a defense research establishment comparable to the American one. Accordingly, they could not draw on a pool of Cold War–created talent to develop an IT industry in its commercial phase. Small wonder that they did not and the Americans did.

Comparisons of *Fortune* 500 listings are one way to prove the sustainability of German and Japanese firms. Another and perhaps even better yardstick is the performance of small and medium enterprises (SMEs). Japanese SMEs are famous because of their supplier role in big-firm vertical networking (*kereitsu*). Many of them followed the big Japanese automobile assemblers to the US to form part of supplier chains for Japanese US transplants. SMEs in a *kereitsu* worked intimately with the large firms in the development and manufacture of parts. The 40,000 firms in the Toyota Production System, for example, had long-term relations with the firm. They operated as a supplier "club," an arena for information exchange between buyers and suppliers (as well, of course, as a source of capital). Supplier firms worked closely with their "customers," i.e., within Toyota, in product development to meet their specific needs. That is, suppliers did their own product research and development, calling on the knowhow and information network of their customers (Toyota) in these efforts. The sustained participation of SMEs in Japanese manufacturing is an integral part of any explanation of Japan's long-term manufacturing prowess.

German SMEs, which they call the *Mittelstand* (composed primarily of family-owned firms with sales of up to €1 billion), probably contributed more to the nation's prosperity than Germany's *Fortune* 500 companies, although with the metrics used in America that contribution is hard to detect. American commentators have stressed low German growth rates of 2.1 percent between 1994 and 2004, low domestic consumer demand, and low investment levels recorded in banks and investment circles. They therefore concluded that the German economy was the "sick man of Europe." The head of General Motors Europe was so pessimistic about Germany's economic future that he gloomily proclaimed: for General Motors it is "out of Germany or out of business" (Vernohr and Meyer, 2007, 29; Simon, 1996).

The remark might have been true for GM's car business in the German market, but it did not apply to the marketing of German-manufactured products globally. German firms earned the greatest export surpluses in the world ($200 billion in 2006), ahead even of China and Japan. German *Fortune* 500 companies could claim much credit for this achievement, but so could German SMEs. The latter were a driving force behind the rebirth of the German economy in the 1950s and 1960s and continued to be thereafter. At the century's close, 340,000

German SMEs produced goods and services exported to foreign countries; 100,000 of them had direct foreign investment in networks and installations that supported their export operations. These firms exported 40 percent of all German manufactured goods – a major contribution to Germany's constant huge trade surpluses.

From the perspective of a US finance professor, the performance of German SMEs is hard to measure. SMEs were/are mainly family-owned and self-financed. Stock-market-driven short-term financial data, therefore, are not available. Nor can they be evaluated with regard to management forms. US start-ups are famous for turning themselves, after a successful period of initial growth, into public corporations that operate under professional management. Founders get very rich this way, but from increasing stock valuations, not profits from business activity. Data about rates and successes of initial public offering (IPO) conversions are not of much help when evaluating the performance of German SME firms, however, because they remain, by family choice, under family ownership from generation to generation. The conversion rate of these quite successful firms into publicly owned companies through IPOs is very low.

Family-owned German businesses are not victims of leveraged buyouts by private equity companies. In Germany between 2000 and 2007 only 1 percent of successor arrangements for founder- or family-run firms involved private equity buyouts (Schmohl, 2009, 4). Takeovers by foreign private equity firms are particularly disliked. "Although many family businesses are going through generational changes," Josh Kosman writes, "... few have sold out to foreign Private Equity firms" (Kosman, 2010, 168). Germany ranks lowest among the European countries with regard to foreign private equity buyouts. In 2005, the Social Democratic Party chairman Franz Müntefering compared these private equity firms, which flourish in the US under favorable tax laws, to locusts, saying "they graze on underpriced businesses, lay off employees, and move on" (Kosman, 2010, 168).

Nor can judgments about SME performance be made indirectly through, for example, information about a family-owned firm's adoption of professional management. Germany's SMEs try to avoid the Buddenbrooks effect (having incompetent offspring take over from competent founders) by hiring professional managers. But the firms do not adopt the outlook of a professional management caste like that in the US. Instead, they usually operate under hybrid management (family plus professional managers) as a result of which they profit from management expertise while the firm's metrics are set by owner families not managers – especially not US-style managers who engage in short-term profit maximization and cost cutting at the expense of the workforce.

Rather, German family-owned SMEs give priority to the sustainability of the firm as an extended family within a valued community. The factors supporting this goal become their all-important metrics. Because German *Mittelstand* firms make implicit lifetime commitments to their employees, the latter need to be more than competent. The firms carefully recruit and train skilled people, relying on an apprenticeship–master system inherited from the past, complemented by an excellent technical and commercial school system. Since manufacturers know that sustainability demands staying abreast if not ahead in technology, the firms invest 5 percent of their revenues into research and development (Vernohr and Meyer, 2007, 29). They also exploit available scientific knowledge and knowhow by working with people in universities and polytechnics (*Fachhochschulen*), research institutes, and special places such as the Fraunhofer Institutes set up all over Germany to facilitate the transfer of scientific research into innovative products and services in firms. To promote worldwide success in niche services and manufacturing, on which they concentrate, German SMEs devote much time to cultivating customer relations, owners often making repeated foreign trips in order to establish and maintain personal contacts with customers.

US managerialism and finance capitalism

Beginning in the 1980s the US management caste increasingly worked with corporate lawyers, stockholders, and financial promoters in various kinds of deal making. Some in the caste subjected quite successful public firms to leveraged buyout schemes that converted them into private equity companies. Only firms with significant untapped borrowing capacity, undervalued assets, and high cash flows – "common characteristics of many, if not most, of America's largest and more prosperous corporations" (Shad, 1984, 6) – could get involved because buyouts were financed from money borrowed on a target company's own credit line, and the huge debt incurred was paid back from a target company's own cash flow (Kosman, 2010). These deals made money for institutional investment funds that lent the money (e.g. public employees' pension plans), for the deal makers, for the target company shareholders (who received 50 percent to 100 percent premiums over the current market price of their stock), and for managers, who were given golden handshakes. But the buyouts did not do much for stakeholders in the target firms.

Other deal makers targeted firms in economic trouble, especially older firms with high legacy costs (fixed pensions and benefits for retirees), in which management sought to shed the fixed costs in a variety of legal ways provided for in takeovers, mergers, and chapter eleven bankruptcies.

Undoubtedly in this endeavor the management caste's desire to break pension and benefit agreements motivated it the most. Defined-benefit private pension plans, entered into during the pre-1980 era of "trust," were the biggest cost problem. There were 112,000 of these in the US in 1983, each guaranteeing fixed levels of income to retirees. Many were not fully funded, that is, management, pressed by stockholder desires for good quarterly income statements and dividends to keep the stock price high, had made funding the employee pension plan a low priority. Tough-minded managers preferred to eliminate pension and benefit plans altogether, or, failing that, to move employees into undefined contribution schemes that did not guarantee fixed incomes for retirees, or to have them establish individual pension savings accounts that greatly reduced company contributions and obligations.

Undefined benefit plans and individual savings accounts permitted management variously to lower the benefit amounts, to borrow from their employees' individual accounts, to pressure workers to put company stock into their personal retirement accounts, or to manipulate a plan's fund in ways that let a company appear to be more profitable than it actually was. In these schemes, the workers usually assumed all of the risks the companies suffered from stock and bond market declines. Financial institutions, too, preferred undefined contribution and individual savings account plans, because fees for managing them were high – typically 2 to 4 percent of a worker's contribution, a significant reduction in his or her pension, although a steady stream of income for financial institutions managing the accounts.

The ruthless, relentless, and radical transformation of private pension plans that the management caste carried out at the end of the twentieth century broke up the moral order that had been created in postwar America. "From Reagan through [George W.] Bush," Jack Rasmus reported in 2004, corporations have been terminating and undermining group pension plans by shutting down plants and moving companies, underfunding the plans, diverting funds to other corporate use when they can get away with it, and then, when the plan is in jeopardy, with the assistance of government and the courts, funneling whatever remains into 401-K type personal savings plans. From the passage of the Employee Retirement Income Security Act (ERISA) in 1974 until 2003, more than 160,000 Defined Benefits plans have gone under in the US. (Rasmus, 2004, 3)

During the same time the number of personal retirement accounts mushroomed. Very few households had such accounts in 1982, but by 1995 23 percent of households had a 401-K or an equivalent individual retirement account. That percentage reached 67 in 2004. The management caste, allied with friends in Congress and the Oval Office, carried through this radical transformation of private pension planning to the great detriment of employees everywhere in America (Munnell et al., 2008).

Management justifies its behavior in all this on practical grounds: it is looking after shareholder interests. Those who terminated legacy costs even became management heroes, like Richard S. Miller, CEO of Bethlehem Steel, who jettisoned the company's $3.7 billion unfunded pension obligation to its retirees. This obligation removed, venture capitalist Wilbur L. Ross bought the firm, combined it with four other derelict steel firms, and then sold the amalgamated firm, which had cost him $400 million to buy, for $4.5 billion (Walsh, 2005). What a guy!

Here the issue once again is metrics. The language that managers and business school academics use in articles about restructuring, mergers, acquisitions, leveraged buyouts and the like rarely, if ever, touches on how employees are affected – other than to mention as an afterthought that rumors of these deals affect employee morale and retention and must be managed carefully. Most discussion focuses on stockholder benefits, profits, and stock market valuation, before and after the deal, and on firm survival rates. These are the concerns of people in the proprietary firm; and it is they who determine judgments about agency conflict. Since an entity conception of the firm is not in their consciousness, they as management scientists care little about what happens to the firm's employees or retirees. Moreover, they do not look for entity solutions to these problems because employees are not integral to management structures. It is the management caste's show, with the unions kept on the outside. "What bothered Mr. Conway, the union leader [at the demise of Bethlehem Steel]," *New York Times* reporter M. W. Walsh wrote,

> was not so much Mr. Ross's inability to wring more money out of the pension system or his remarkable profit on the deal. What troubled him, he said, was that the country seemed unable to take any lessons away from the demise of the steel companies and how it affected so many working people. "It just staggers us that America's not caught on to what's happening to it," he said. (Walsh, 2005, 4)

Japanese and German systems of ownership and governance in private firms would never have cooperated and never in fact did cooperate with financiers and brokerage firms to bringing about such despoliation of their employees as happened under managerialism in the United States.

Business schools and the derivatives market

Before we consider the relation between business schools and derivatives trading, two aspects of management that are not directly connected to business schools have to be mentioned, because they permitted hedge fund operators and investment bankers to mobilize money on an unprecedented scale. Michael

Lewis, in *The Big Short*, writes about the first aspect. In 1981 John Gutfreund transformed Solomon Brothers from a private partnership into Wall Street's first public corporation. Thereafter, most private partnerships followed suit. At the point at which the private investment bank became a public corporation the firm became a black box, meaning that the shareholders, who in a public corporation finance the risk taking, had very little idea of what the risk takers – the traders working in the firm – were doing because they were remote from and had no understanding of what went on daily in the firm. And what they, the risk takers, were doing was leveraging the corporation's balance sheets with exotic risks that inflated their and management's bonuses and compensation disproportionately to what stockholders received, thereby creating the agency conflict that often accompanies managerialism. Lewis claims that with the separation of ownership from management, the psychological foundation "of Wall Street shifted, from trust to blind faith." And a misplaced faith at that. "No investment bank owned by its employees," he wrote,

> would have leveraged itself 35-1, or bought and held $50 billion in mezzanine [high risk] CDOs [Collateralized Debt Obligations]. I doubt any partnership would have sought to game the rating agencies, or leap into bed with loan sharks, or even allow mezzanine CDOs to be sold to its customers. The short-term expected gains would not have justified the long-term expected loss. (Lewis, 2010, 258)

The conversion of private investment banks into public corporations, then, increased moral hazard, since it enabled the management caste to avoid taking full responsibility for its actions, to act in fact less responsibly than it should, and to shove off its responsibility onto other parties (buyer beware).

The second enabler was the institutional investor. Large investors, for example employee pension funds and insurance companies, whose managers were themselves quantifiers, not only urged corporate management to keep stock prices high, but they looked for investment opportunities that would maximize their income flows. Hedge funds and financial investment firms liked to deal with institutional investors who had billions at their disposal. With institutional investors buying uncritically, transactions in questionable financial derivatives from highly leveraged investment traders reached the startling volumes that Robert Johnson reported in his testimony before Congress.

Constructing the vehicle of greed

The preeminent pioneer in finance mathematics was probably Harry Markowitz, a Chicago student and eventual winner of the Nobel Prize in economics, who used quantitative methods to show how investors can maximize returns and lower their risks by diversifying their portfolios. But the massive development of the derivatives market proceeded not from this but from three other significant academic events. The first occurred in 1969 when Robert Merton introduced stochastic calculus into the study of finance; the second took place in 1973 with the publication of the Black-Scholes Formula for Pricing European Calls and Puts; the third occurred in 1981 when Harrison-Plasma used the general theory of continuous-time stochastic processes to put the Black-Scholes option pricing formula on a solid theoretical footing, and consequently demonstrated how to price numerous other derivatives (Korn, 2010). This permitted mathematics to be used in all four branches of finance mathematics: modeling, optimal investment calculations, option pricing, and risk management. Thereafter, trading in derivatives could be modeled and market behavior could be reasonably predicted.

Although these were considerable individual achievements (for which Merton and Scholes won Nobel Prizes in economics in 1997 – Black was by then deceased), their impact really resulted from the introduction of the New Look into economics departments and business schools during the Ford Foundation-sponsored curricula reform in the 1960s. The intellectual precedents of the New Look are direct and unmistakable. As described in Chapter 1, the new paradigm began in operations research in World War Two, invaded schools of industrial administration immediately thereafter, from whence it spread into the social sciences. The academic careers of three professors involved in the significant events just mentioned tracked this development pattern. Robert Merton, who earned a bachelor of science degree in engineering mathematics at Columbia and a master of science at the California Institute of Technology, migrated into economics from engineering when he wrote a doctoral dissertation at the Massachusetts Institute of Technology under Paul Samuelson, who had himself drawn on OR when he applied linear programming equations (developed for operations research at the Rand Corporation) to neoclassical marginal analysis.

Stanley R. Pliska's and J. Michael Harrison's careers followed the path from operations research into social science even more directly. Both did PhDs in OR at Stanford University, Harrison in 1970, and Pliska in 1972, before moving into mathematical finance, Harrison at Stanford's Graduate School of Business, and Pliska in the business school at the University of Illinois, Chicago Circle. Accordingly, their first job experiences and academic papers handled typical OR problems; only later did their interest shift to quantitative analysis of derivative markets in a landmark collaboration.

Myron Scholes and Fischer Black did not start in operations research. A Canadian, Scholes earned a BA in economics at McMaster's University, where his professors introduced him to the work of two future Nobel Prize winners, George Stigler and

Milton Friedman. Scholes attended the University of Chicago business school, where he studied with Eugene Fama, Michael Jensen, and Merton Miller, among others, then developing the field of finance economics. Scholes received a PhD from Chicago in 1969, a year after having taken a position at MIT's Sloan School, where he knew Black. Sloan School, as a school of industrial engineering, had been preoccupied with OR during and after World War Two. For his part, Black studied for his PhD under Marvin Minsky at MIT (although the degree was granted in applied mathematics at Harvard University). He worked in 1971 at the University of Chicago Booth School of Business before returning to MIT's Sloan School to work with Scholes. It was a pretty small club who handed out Nobel Prizes to each other.

When Markowitz, Jensen, Black, Scholes, Harrison, and Pliska started in the 1960s, no field of finance mathematics yet existed; they helped create one, but, as we have seen, not from scratch. It emerged from postwar operations research and spread into the social sciences during the Ford Foundation's campaign to upgrade the mathematical content of US top business school curricula, in order for management studies to become a respected scientific discipline (Locke, 1989; Khurana, 2007).

This theoretical work did not cause the recent meltdown in financial markets in 2007–2008, but without it, the massive throughput of transactions that raised markets to unbelievable heights and then brought them down could not have occurred. For the models these professors developed allowed Wall Street to price trillions of dollars' worth of derivatives rationally in a market system thought of as an orderly, independent, continuous process. That was the presumption of the Capital Asset Pricing Model (CAPM) that Markowitz introduced, and about which Lawrence Mitchell recently wrote:

[T]he product of a regression analysis called *beta*, CAPM allows investors to build the kinds of potentially lower-risk, higher-return portfolios ... described by Markowitz, based solely upon a narrow range of information about the stock. The business itself matters little, if at all. All an investor needs is *beta*. No balance sheet, no profit and loss statement, no cash flow information, no management analysis of its performance and plans, no sense of corporate direction, no knowledge of what is on its research and development pipeline, no need even to know what products the corporation makes or what services it provides. Just *beta*. The stock is virtually independent of the corporation that issued it. CAPM has been adopted and is daily used by countless stock analysts and institutional money managers. Almost every American who invests in the market through mutual funds or other institutional media has invested on the basis of CAPM. (Mitchell, 2007, 275)

That was also the presumption of the Black-Scholes formula. According to that formula, stock prices move, as mathematicians put it, in a "random walk," in continuous time that allows investors to determine the relevant probabilities for volatility. How high or low a stock or option would move in a certain time frame could now be predicted based on the law of large numbers. "Quantitative traders ... came to see the model," Patterson observed, "as a reflection of how the market actually worked. The model soon became so ubiquitous that ... it became difficult to tell the difference between the model and the market itself" (Patterson, 2010, 39).

Such theories were a great boon to finance studies in business schools. They spawned more and more professorships in mathematical finance, the pursuit of new types of products such as exotic options, credit derivatives, equity-linked notes, the forging of new fields that combined computation with theoretical knowledge, for example, Monte Carlo methods, random numbers, parallelization, Malliavin calculus, copulax, nonlinear optimization, filling problems, and in general the pushing of research that focused on computational finance, phynance, quantitative finance, and interdisciplinarity, while grappling with interesting theoretical problems, such as the valuation of exotic options, risk measurement theory, and equivalent martingale theory.

On the instructional level, the need for quantitative analysts prompted the schools in a very short time to develop specialized master's and PhD courses in financial engineering, mathematical finance, and computational finance – and to create new degrees. Cass Business School near London's financial district introduced quantitative finance programs. It established an MSc. in quantitative finance, an MSc. in financial mathematics and an MSc. in mathematical trading and finance. In the UK, Paul Wilmott taught the first mathematical finance course at Oxford University. Afterwards he developed the largest European training program in London, a one-year course that led to a widely respected Certificate in Quantification Finance.

Not surprisingly, because it had been a leader under Dean Bach in developing the Ford Foundation's program after World War Two, Carnegie Institute of Technology's Graduate School of Industrial Administration (to become the Tepper School of Business in 2003) set up a Financial Analyst Security Trading Center (FAST) in 1989, one of the first US educational institutions to replicate successfully the live international data feeds and sophisticated software of Wall Street trading firms (Bach, 1958). The business school at Carnegie Mellon introduced an MBA in computational finance, an MS in quantitative economics and an MS in computation finance in which the students studied equities, bond portfolio management, and the stochastic models upon which derivatives trading is based. Although early off the mark, there was nothing exceptional in the last decade of the twentieth century about the program in mathematical finance at Carnegie Mellon; all the top business schools developed them.

Professors at these schools, moreover, were not shy about establishing contacts with people in praxis. Milton Friedman, for example, lobbied for the establishment of an options exchange in Chicago. On April 26, 1975, a month before the Black-Scholes paper appeared, the Chicago Board of Options Exchange opened. Texas Instruments made a hand calculator that priced options using the Black-Scholes formula. Black, whose preoccupation with derivatives started while working for Arthur D. Little, which earlier had developed a great interest in OR, took a job with Goldman Sachs in 1984 designing derivatives architecture (Magee, 2002). Professor Emanuel Derman, head of mathematical finance at Columbia University, worked at Goldman Sachs with Black. These examples illustrate the symbiotic relationship that developed between business school professors and people in praxis (Chan, 2010).

For people in praxis to collaborate with business school finance professors in model building and product design is one thing, but why turn actual trading in hedge funds and investment banks over to a bunch of mathematics geeks who knew almost nothing about finance? The answer is that the geeks' models made money and lots of it. Quantification added volume, speed, and spread to market trading, which raised it to a higher dimension of trading experience. As Scott Patterson phrased it, "the quants creat[ed] a massive electronic network, a digitized, computerized money trading machine that could shift billions around the globe in the blink of an eye, at the click of a mouse" (Patterson, 2010, 119; see also Bowley, 2011). Patterson dubbed the system "The Money Grid." Three illustrations of how it worked verify his point.

The first illustration is Peter Muller's Process Driven Trading (PDT) unit organized and operated inside the Morgan Stanley building on the Avenue of the Americas in New York City. There Muller assembled a team of math and computer specialists – Kim Elsesser, a programmer with a master's degree in operations research from MIT, Mike Reed, a PhD in electrical engineering from Princeton, Ken Nickerson, with a degree in operations research from Stanford, Amy Wong, with a master's in electrical engineering from MIT, and Shakil Ahmed, a programming talent from Yale. This PDT group constructed an automatic trading machine they called Midas. Nickerson and Ahmed trolled for market signals that would tell the computer which stocks to buy and sell, with Nickerson concentrating on US markets and Ahmed on those overseas. Reed created a supercomputer infrastructure that plugged into markets around the world. Later, Jaipal Tuttle, a PhD in physics from the University of California at Santa Cruz, joined them. Tuttle's knowledge of physics permitted the group to understand many of the complex trades PDT did.

The strategy at first was statistical arbitrage. Arbitrage involves buying an asset in one market and almost simultaneously selling that asset in another. If gold is trading for $1,000 in New York, and for $1,050 in London, the dealer buys the commodity in New York and sells it in London, and pockets the $50 difference. The strategy's success requires an ability to do this instantaneously (which has been possible since the era of the telegraph and the telephone) and to find the pricing discrepancies between markets from which a dealer can profit, which heretofore was not easy to do. Therefore, arbitrage was not as profitable an activity in investment banking until the word statistical was added to it, because that allowed APT to harness the speed, volume, and spread capacity of Midas to arbitrage trading. Later PDT expanded its activities into Eurodollars and energy futures, with bonds and options. "Whatever they could model, they would trade" (Patterson, 2010, 129).

Between 1996 and 2006, PDT earned $4 billion in profits. Since the group received 20 percent of these profits, a handful of people earned a billion dollars. The salaries of these young people in some years exceeded the take-home pay of Morgan Stanley's top executives, who themselves benefitted handsomely from the unit's trading through the firm's bonus system. In the late 1990s and early 2000s PDT accounted for 25 percent of the parent firm's net income.

The second illustration of this pattern is the Citadel Hedge Fund based in Chicago. In 1994 there were 1,945 hedge funds, that is, private groups of wealthy investors; by 1998 the number had grown to 7,500. The Citadel Investment Group started trading on November 1, 1990 in Chicago with $4.6 million in capital. It specialized in using mathematical models to discover deals in the market for convertible bonds. By 1992 the firm had sixty employees and $200 million in capital. By 1994 it had 1 billion dollars under management and had started to branch out into statistical arbitrage and the marketing of subprime mortgages. By 1998 Citadel sat on top of $6 billion, and was the sixth-largest hedge fund in the world. It was also turning into a hedge fund factory, hiring new managers to set them up. The year 2002 saw energy trading added, and a team of quantifiers built commodity pricing models to ramp up trading operations in that sector. The firm hired meteorologists to deal with supply-and-demand issues that could impact energy prices. By 2005 Citadel employed seventy-two PhDs, including mathematicians and astrophysicists, who worked in the firm's Quantitative Research Group. The group had a huge mainframe computer, connected with world markets and the hedge fund's other offices in London, Tokyo, and New York. By the end of 2007 Citadel had $140 billion in gross assets with which to trade (mostly borrowed) and $15 billion of its own capital. The firm was then leveraged at a 9 to 1 ratio, which enabled it to inflate profits, but this was not excessive leverage compared to the high risk exposure of other funds. In fifteen years Citadel's trading turned its head, Ken Griffins, and his chief lieutenants, into billionaires, and its other employees into wealthy people.

The third illustration of this pattern is American International Group Financial Products (AIG-FP). Howard Sosin and Randy Rackson, an MBA from the Wharton School, started AIG's financial products unit in 1987 to trade over the counter in derivatives markets worldwide. The unit, using sophisticated computer models, prospered. By 1993, when Sosin left to make a fortune elsewhere, the unit had 125 employees and an annual profit of $100 million. Thomas Savage, a PhD in mathematics from Claremont Graduate School, took over, with the same prosperous results. The financial products unit between 1987 and 2004 added $5 billion to AIG's pre-tax income and made a major contribution to increasing the parent firm's market capitalization from $11 billion to $181 billion. The AIG share price rose in the same period from $5.53 to $63.34.

Then AIG-FP made two strategic mistakes. In 1998, J. P. Morgan asked the insurance giant to cover its entire portfolio. Gary Gorton, Professor at Yale University, who helped set up the financial unit's computer model, ran the numbers and concluded that if they made the deal with J. P. Morgan, there was a 99.5 percent chance that AIG would never have to pay out. The insurance contract, called in the business a credit default swap, was the first CDS the firm did. There would be many more.

Secondly, AIG-FP decided to insure (issue CDSs for) residential-mortgage-backed securities (called collateralized debt obligations, CDOs). To shrewd observers in the mortgage business, subprime housing mortgages were not a good investment, but there was money to be made from them when mortgages defaulted. In 2000, of the $130 billion subprime mortgage contracts concluded in the US, $55 billion had been packaged in mortgage bonds, which the rating agencies had designated

Triple A (low risk). By 2005, the amount in subprime mortgages had ballooned to $625 billion, of which investment bankers had repackaged $507 billion into Triple A–rated mortgage bonds. Despite the ratings, these CDOs were highly toxic securities because 80 percent of the packages were risky subprime mortgages.

The trick for clever traders: buy as many high-risk subprime-loaded real estate CDOs as possible, insure them as credit default swaps, and wait for subprime mortgagees to default on their loans – at which point the bondholders would not lose because the bonds were insured. Gorton built the model at AIG-FP that priced CDOs, and the firm – a victim of its own statistical model – decided to buy massively into them. By 2005 AIG-FP had issued CDSs for $80 billion of real-estate-backed CDOs. Lower-middle-class subprime mortgagees began to default heavily on their loans, which caused the CDOs in which they had been packaged rapidly to lose value.

According to CDS contracts with AIG-FP, if the underlying insured asset declined for whatever reason, the insurance provider (AIG) had to put up more collateral since the risk of default had grown. In August 2007 Goldman Sachs asked AIG for $1.5 billion to cover the value loss in its AIG-insured mortgage-backed securities. In October it asked for another $2 billion. Then Goldman Sachs demanded an extra $8 billion to $9 billion in collateral from AIG-FP. That provoked a fatal model failure. Only the massive inputs of Troubled Asset Relief Program (TARP) funds from the federal government rescued the firm.

When, in October 2008, Gerry Pasciucco, vice chairman at Morgan Stanley, arrived at AIG-FP to take over, he found $2.7 trillion in CDS contracts, 50,000 outstanding trades, with 2,000 firms on the books. Because AIG-FP's collapse affected the parent firm, AIG stock had become almost worthless. The dealmakers, however, left with hefty bonuses and severance pay. Joseph Cassano, who headed AIG-FP until February 2008, received $46.6 million in salary and bonuses in 2006 and $24.6 million in 2007 – another example of managerialism at work in public corporations with managers the winners and stockholders the losers.

Although these three operations are different in specificities, they are particularly good examples of how mathematical modeling, programming, and the internet combined to raise derivatives trading to another dimension. They are, therefore, not exceptional in the sense that they fit into the money grid that drove international investor capitalism, one from which business school research into mathematical finance, and the stream of graduates the schools sent into praxis, profited.

Denouement

The speed, volume, and spread that account for the remarkable growth in derivative trading rested on feet of clay. Federal Reserve chairman Alan Greenspan's prediction that markets self-correct was not true; sometimes they self-destruct. The latter does not happen frequently. Past experience, even during the Great Depression, proved that markets recover from meltdowns. But the unprecedented speed, volume, and spread that derivative trading reached in the interconnected IT world presaged, if things really did go wrong, a collapse that would mirror the intensity of the preceding upswing and suck the liquidity out of financial institutions, leaving the economy without financial underpinning. Why would things fall apart?

There were doubters about finance models just as there had been about operations research models after World War Two. Nonmathematicians outside the OR citadel had disliked the quantifiers, as had the old-guard finance people in academia and in Wall Street investment banking. More important, doubts also arose within the ranks of finance mathematicians just as they had earlier in the ranks of OR scientists in the pages of the *Journal of the Operational Research Society*. Benoist Mandelbrot detected the flaw in Chicago Business School Professor Eugene Fama's Efficiency Market Hypothesis and the Black-Scholes pricing formula before they were even announced (Cootner, 1964). His studies of cotton prices and income distribution revealed wildly disparate leaps in prices that did not follow theories of predictable market behavior. He published the findings ("The Variation of Certain Speculative Prices") in an internal research memo at IBM. Then he worked out an alternative method to measure the erratic behavior of prices, based on the mathematics he learned in Paris under Paul Lévy. Mandelbrot's essay struck at the heart of the quantification revolution because he challenged the core idea the revolution had advanced – that the market moved in tiny incremental predictable ticks. Ignoring Mandelbrot, Wall Street quantifiers decided to adopt strategies based on the Black-Scholes formula in order to shelter their highly leveraged ventures in derivative trading.

Nonetheless, Mandelbrot's critique could not be ignored because his was not just an academic exercise. Although top US business school professors and their students in investment firms shelved his views (they were "too messy" and "too chaotic"), the traders had to confront market reality on Black Monday, October 29, 1987, when a market plunge wiped out the savings and loan industry. (It was after Howard Sosin lost his job in that debacle that he started AIG-FP.) The event prompted Nassim Taleb to become another determined critic of mathematical finance market models. He stated that investors who believed markets moved according to a random walk and are, consequently, statistically predictable are "fooled by randomness" (Taleb, 2001, 2010; Patterson, 2010, 59). There are wild, unexpected swings in markets, which he called "Black Swans." If mathematics-schooled traders used models based on historical trends and expectations of a random walk (models of predictable pricing), it would lead them to disaster. And there are "more Black Swans out there than people think."

In the summer of 1998, the mathematicians running a massive hedge fund known as Long-Term Capital Management, operating on "sophisticated computer models and risk management strategies and using 'unfathomable' amounts of leverage," encountered a Black Swan. The firm lost billions and the episode nearly destabilized global markets.

The century turned, more financial analysts joined people in the post-autistic economics protest against neoclassical economics, of which the mathematical revolution in finance was an offshoot. Because of Black Swans, the critics of financial mathematics had perhaps a greater sense of urgency in their specific protest than regular students of economics. Paul Wilmott, a leading figure in the finance quantification movement, worried particularly about a financial system blow-up. In 2002, his paper in *The Philosophical Transactions of the Royal Society* stated: "It is clear that a major rethink is desperately required if the world is to avoid a mathematical-led meltdown … [Financial markets were once run by the] old boy network but lately only those with PhDs in mathematics or physics are considered suitable to master the complexities of the financial market" (Patterson, 2010, 292).

When the crisis came, more financial analysts questioned fundamental assumptions behind the finance mathematics project. In January 2009, Wilmott and Emanuel Derman issued The Financial Modelers Manifesto, which opened with words reminiscent of Karl Marx: "A specter is haunting markets – the specter of illiquidity, frozen credit, and the failure of financial models." Then followed the great doubt:

Physics, because of its astonishing success at predicting the future behavior of material objects from their present state, has inspired most financial modeling. Physicists study the world by repeating the same experiments over and over again to discover forces and their almost magical mathematical laws ... It's a different story with finance and economics, which are concerned with the mental world of monetary value. Financial theory has tried hard to emulate the style and elegance of physics in order to discover its own laws ... The truth is that there are no fundamental laws in finance. (Financial Modelers Manifesto, 2009; Dobbin and Jung, 2010)

Finance mathematicians rarely blame themselves for crises. Mathematics is a formal science that depends on the clarity and accuracy of inputs for applicability. Nonetheless, financial mathematicians had naïvely sent misleading signals to nonmathematicians in the investment community, which had induced the belief that everything can be modeled. They had glorified simplistic modeling as state-of-the-art; they had thought about risk measures and forgot about risk management (Korn, 2010).

These admissions have broad implications for this historical inquiry because they question once again the wisdom of the Ford Foundation project that introduced unbounded rationality in the form of neoclassical economics into business and economics curricula in the 1960s. Already in the late 1970s, OR scientist Russell Ackoff, head of Operations Research at the Wharton School, drew negative conclusions about the suitability of mathematical models for management decision-making. This, however, did not stop quantitative analysts in finance, many of whom came from operations research and should, therefore, have known better, from following the same mathematical will-o'-the-wisp that the previous generation of OR enthusiasts had followed postwar – and experiencing the same disillusionment twenty-five years after Ackoff, for the shortcomings now recognized in mathematical models for decision making in financial markets are similar to those often acknowledged in the operations research community decades before.

At bottom, the attempt to turn management into a positivist science seems to have misfired. It might have won Nobel Prizes for professors and set them to work on mounds of research, published in academic journals and taught in MBA classrooms, but from a management point of view so much investment in the creation of a positivist management science in business schools has not, to use their jargon, been "cost effective." It might have been better to have devoted the money and the time in business school education to the human aspect of management and to have left the number crunching to people in natural science and technology.

What about the moral dimension in the education of this elite? Since Immanuel Kant observed that science had nothing to do with ethics, neither mathematical financial analysts nor their professors in business schools have been hampered by ethical restraints. As for Wall Street and the City of London, the old boys' network might at one time have lived up to the image of trust based on a handshake and a "gentleman's word is his bond," but since the institutional investors have taken over, the stockholders in publicly owned investment banks have proven to be unable to control their managers' risk appetite, and government regulators demonstrate ineffectuality at every turn. The absence of a moral order in the finance world has been patently obvious. Or, as Louis Lesce, who worked at Chase Manhattan Bank for decades, wrote: "There is no moral crisis on the Street because there is no morality there" (email to Locke, December 23, 2010).

The problem is that speed, volume, and spread increase the dimension of evil. The heightened intensity and dimension of trade do not present a moral problem so much because young quantitative finance analysts earned obscene amounts of money, while others suffered. Americans believe in the right of everyone to "make it big." They are not resented; they are the heroes of democratic capitalism. Nor is it particularly a moral problem if the modelers are wrong. They assume no moral responsibility for the outcomes if the Black-Scholes formula or Professor Fama's efficiency-market hypothesis are incorrect. Scientific outcomes are never definitive.

There is, however, a great moral wrong that quantitative analysts have done. They have taken high-risk derivatives (Triple B–rated securities) and stacked them into financial packages that, under their coaxing, rating firms have designated Triple A risks, that is no risk, and then sold as such to pension plans, insurance companies, and other institutional investors all over the world. They have created their own derivative world, without much reference in fact to business and industry, and sold it to the investor public. This action precipitated the subprime mortgage crisis in 2007 and the general financial systems breakdown that followed. Unmistakably, business school professors and finance mathematicians who designed these packages knew that what they were doing was, if not fraudulent, at least highly immoral, and they did it on a massive scale (Adams and Smith, 2010).

Nothing in business school education set up moral barriers to their doing this because the ethical solution, as J. M. Bernstein points out, is not to be found in individual motivation but in effective collective action, and to think that it can take place without institutions to constrain it is an illusion (Bernstein, 2010). Adam Smith said that the pursuit of self-interest in the marketplace promotes the general interest (the good), but Professor Bernstein says that self-interest (profit taking) in financial firms cannot be a "good" unless their market trades are involved in wealth creation. Since they are not, and business schools are doing nothing institutionally to promote financial markets as wealth-creating entities, business school talk about ethics is a concoction of fantasy.

Back to balance

Throughout the ages, the idea of management, that is, of getting things done through people in organizations, has been accepted as a perfectly normal function. Not only does this study agree with that, but it affirms that organizations are essential to modern societies and the managers who run them are a vital part of modern living. But the notion that a management caste should be allowed to run things is much more problematic, and the further notion that a special class of business schools should be devoted to educating such a caste is even more problematic. Americans are used to these ideas because they grew out of the specificity of American historical experience. Yet managerialism and US business schools, which Americans proselytized throughout the developed and developing world, are responsible for creating lives out of balance within the United States and internationally in the last quarter of the twentieth century. This conclusion reviews the indictment and then briefly discusses reform guidelines that might help remedy the harm that has been done.

The view that management is a general function was not readily accepted anywhere outside the US. A person does not just manage. Rather, he/she manages a hat factory, a steel mill, a department store, a railway company. In the nineteenth century, informed foreigners recognized that a different idea was developing in the US. Professor Alois Riedler, of the Technical Institute of Charlottenburg (Berlin), after touring American industries at the time of the Chicago World's Fair (1893), pointed out the real message that American industrialization had for German engineers:

> To that which I think we can learn from American industrial life I would like to add that there is not much to learn in technology. American mechanical construction ... workshops are in many ways unbelievably backward ... And the same goes for a large percentage of boilermakers ... Overall the technical development is backward: only the economic has been massively developed. But it must not be confused with technical progress, which is very modest and cannot be compared with our own. (Riedler, 1894, 17–18)

Riedler realized, long before Taylor was ever heard of in Europe, from whence the American challenge came. Others, especially after Taylor and his American disciples appeared, awoke to the "American danger;" Paul Müller, of the German Engineering Association (VDI), spent seven months in America before World War One studying management in the mechanical industry (Homburg, 1978, 174–75). That "American danger," he found, was management, which developed into the subject of this book: managerialism.

The academic content of US business schools, in their infancy, was not scientifically mature, but the schools, as management institutions, started to participate in executive education programs in which the military participated, as the general management idea became omnipresent after 1917. Charles de Gaulle in 1934 pinpointed the originality of the interplay between general management education and the military in American mobilization preparation:

[E]ach one of the service corps is assisted by a permanent study committee formed from the business world, which directly aids it … The Americans have taken steps to assure that both sides (military and industry) have the right personnel. The Army Industrial College has been established to give the military officers in the technical services the desired training. Some of them have even been sent to take courses in the Harvard School of Business Administration. (de Gaulle, 1975, 131)

Executive courses developed thereafter to become permanent fixtures in top business school programs, to which not only US managers flocked but also foreign executives, including many from Germany and Japan, immediately after World War Two.

One of them, the German businessman Dr. Ludwig Vaubel, published a book about his experiences in a senior executive course at Harvard (Vaubel, 1952). He was impressed. But when in the winter of 1952–53 he and a group of business and industrial leaders set about organizing a German *Unternehmer-Akademie* (Entrepreneur Academy), they rejected the American business school model for the one at the Henley Management College, which at that time had no contact with academia. Although Vaubel and his fellow German businessmen had found the American example attractive, they feared that a different academic tradition in their country, centered on science, had saddled Germany with scientifically trained (*wissenschaftliche*), inexperienced, praxis-alienated professors – and in *BWL* (business economics) it had. Pragmatically minded German businessmen and industrialists accordingly ignored university business economics (*BWL*) when setting up post-experience management educational programs in Germany. In 1955, when the first Baden-Baden Managers Conference (a regular event thereafter) gathered, groups of senior managers met, as at Henley, for relatively unstructured discussions among themselves about management. The professors were not invited.

That German businessmen, who so benefited from their sojourn at the Harvard Business School, would reject the American business school executive course model appears to be counterintuitive. But the reason is easy to explain – if it is remembered that when they attended Harvard's Senior Executive Seminar, top business schools had not yet been reformed along the lines of the new paradigm. Undergraduate and MBA students in top US business schools at the beginning of the 1950s still learned commercially oriented practical subjects (accounting, merchandizing, etc.) and studied business cases; participants in senior executive courses met primarily to socialize – to learn that they were not isolated economic actors but members of a community that shared some general moral, cultural, and scientific principles, which could be communicated in an in-group setting. There was no claim about their universality – rather these principles might be culturally or historically specific to the region from which the businessmen on the course came. The course allowed their participants to familiarize and socialize as an elite with their peers, in order to acquire the relevant prevailing mores, language and practices of commerce.

The absence of the scientific content that was introduced into top US business schools in the 1960s is precisely what made the Harvard Senior Executive Seminar so attractive to the German businessmen, plus the fact that Harvard Business School professors had business contacts. The fact that already before World War Two, German *BWL* professors pursued the canons of science (*Wissenschaft*) made mixing them with active managers in executive education seminars unattractive, for German managers rejected the view that management could be studied as a science or reduced to one taught by inexperienced academics (Locke, 1984).

The issue that the Germans faced in the early 1950s, American businessmen also faced – with one crucial difference:

there were no business schools in Germany or anywhere else in the world in the 1950s that pretended to educate managers as a generic group and where the curricula for MBAs could be made "scientific." Because management schools existed in the USA and nowhere else, only there in the 1960s was it possible for a group of reformers to set about the education of a general management caste in business schools following a positivist science format.

The principal issue raised in this study, then, has not been whether people in management should learn mathematics, technology, and/or science in school, but whether management, as a general function, can be treated as a rational science in management praxis or in business schools. The answer the book has given is that it cannot, and thinking and acting as if it could has created lives out of balance in the United States and in those parts of the world that American business school education has touched.

As with most complex stories, the failure of science in management did not happen everywhere in the same place at the same time. The problems with operations research and the epistemological debates described in Chapter 1 increased doubts circa 1980 about the usefulness of mathematical model building and mechanical analysis in decision making. Despite the huge amount of investigation precipitated by the Ford and Carnegie funding agencies, despite the evolution of rigorous business school research and its institutionalization, and increased academic incentives attached to the findings, no management science emerged that was of much use in business management or industry, particularly in face of the Japanese industrial challenge. Consequently, some business schools in the United States began to emphasize cultural factors in management studies as early as the 1960s (Thunderbird in Phoenix, Arizona) but especially after the rise of Japan.

Failures in mathematical modeling in OR decision-making, however, did not stop business schools from emphasizing management accounting, financial reporting, and statistical control methods in their core MBA programs – courses of the sort that H. Thomas Johnson denounced in his critique of Management by Results in the US automobile industry. The preoccupation with financial goal-setting in the industry expressed the mindset of the management caste running the companies and of the business schools which sent them graduates. As H. Thomas Johnson, Mike Rother, and other reformers vainly pointed out, none of this helped US manufacturing cope with the challenge of Total Quality Management or respond successfully to the Toyota *kata*.

Instead, top business schools shifted their attention elsewhere. The data on the flow and destination of business school graduates – away from production engineering first, then to consulting, and then to financial services, tracks this flight from manufacturing. But this shift did not mean that, if people in business schools or in automobile management fled economic reality, they behaved more realistically in the finance sector. People in investment firms, banks, and hedge funds confused theory with reality as much as professors of financial economics, committing their businesses to rationality, epitomized in market modeling, the rapid spread of mathematics in finance, and the rise of the institutional investor. Lives spun out of balance when the traders and institutional investors constructed an environment cut off from the company entities where most people work and that make up their socio-economic reality. The shift to finance transformed the way people earned money from socially-beneficial to non-socially-beneficial work pursued in investor capitalism's money grid.

A callous disregard for employee welfare that set in during the 1980s, as the management caste bowed to the dictates of the institutional investor's preoccupation with profits and high stock valuations, gave executives an excuse unilaterally to tear up the tacit social contract that had been made with the previous generation about long-term job security, retirement, and health benefits. It was easy to do, since US management had victoriously asserted the right to manage when confronted with ideas about codetermination and trade unionism. On renouncing this social contract, this leadership caste dissolved the moral order, which justified their monopoly of power in the 1950s, 1960s, and 1970s.

The era of double talk began. Stephen Bainbridge, a law professor concerned with management prerogatives, engaged in it. He claimed that the workers should forget about codetermination and place their hopes for equity in the general expansion of the wealth pie, on the principle that "a rising tide lifts all boats" (Bainbridge, 1998, 67). The empirical evidence for such a reliance is nonexistent, and Bainbridge must have known that. The differential between the pay of top executives and the median pay of their employees never stopped widening after Ronald Reagan took office. By 2009 in the US that differential rose to 208:1 as opposed to 161:1 in 1994. CEOs in Standard & Poor 500 companies received total yearly compensation of $7,500,000 compared to a median total compensation in private sector pay of $36,000 ("The Real Say on Pay," editorial, *New York Times*, September 2, 2010).

The double talk continued. Bainbridge denied employees any right to do something about the income gap. He claimed that, even though America is a democracy, it is not the American tradition to extend that democracy to the workplace. Within the firm-hierarchy, control from the top down is enshrined in American law. With Bainbridge we moved onto George Orwell's *Animal Farm* (1997[1945]), where the management caste, the pigs, have changed the slogan of liberty from "all animals are equal," to "all animals are equal but some animals are more equal than others" – at least in the workplace, where democracy is meaningful only to the rich and powerful.

This double talk invaded American life especially in the age of investor capitalism. People learned that thrift is a virtue, only to be hounded by banks and other lending institutions with a blizzard of offers to use their credit cards – no questions asked. Told that holding a high credit rating is a virtue, people watched mortgage lenders purposely seek out subprime mortgagees, fully expecting them to default on their loans, which hedge fund operators and investment bankers would cynically sell short in order to profit enormously when subprime mortgages failed. Management talks of trust and then acts every day in almost every way to dissolve it. There is no moral compass in which the increasingly depressed, stressed, and unemployed American can believe, no noneconomic institutions (churches, schools, and government) to look to for guidance. What are these other than lives in a world out of balance into which the American people have been dragged kicking and screaming since 1980?

This book blames the business school obsession with numbers for this mistake, that is, the conventional wisdom espoused by post-1945 reformers that management education can be based on a science that improves management performance. But this critique of the science of management is made, especially in the third and fourth chapters, in tandem with a critique of managerialism. Even today most American managers either believe in the superiority of US managerialism or they have become cultural relativists, that is, they think that people might handle management successfully and differently elsewhere than in America but to each his or her own: both work equally well in a specific context, and culturally based systems do not transfer well into other cultures. This book acknowledges the difficulty of transfer, but it also affirms particularly

in Chapter 3 on the automobile industry that management
cultures can migrate – witness the cosmopolitan spread of the
Toyota Production System to the company's facilities everywhere – and in any event a different way of doing things does
not mean equal outcomes. Indeed, low employee dependent
US managerialism does not work as well as high employee
dependent management.

From the firm-entity perspective, to subordinate management
to the constraints of a rationally omniscient business school
view of management science, with decision power lodged in
a management caste, limits the firm's ability to deal effectively
with management problems. Arnd Huchzermeier, who worked
as a consultant in both Germany and America, emphasized this
in an interview in which he evaluated the usefulness in management problem-solving of educational institutions in Germany
and in the US. He stated, with particular reference to US business schools and German faculties of business economics, that
the latter do not possess the concentrated knowledge and skill
of top American business schools (German *BWL* professors
are weaker in mathematics). Consequently, their professors are
usually less capable of translating business problems into formal
systems – not nearly as capable at least as professors in the
premier US business schools. But this comparative deficiency
is not very significant because German *BWL* professors are not
involved in solving business problems but in the teaching of an
academic discipline.

Huchzermeier notes that within German academia plenty of
people have the requisite skills and knowledge needed to trans-
late actual business problems into formal systems; they are just
not concentrated in faculties of business economics as much as
they are dispersed throughout German universities in various
departments and institutes. When brought together from these
various places, the scientists form teams that are quite as capable

as professors in American business schools of formalizing business problems.

Many of them in fact do just that every day. The difference between the Germans and the Americans in this respect is not in knowledge but in knowledge management. The firm, more than academia, is the activating agent that pulls together the requisite skills and knowledge in Germany, and Huchzermeier claims that the German way of concentrating and exploiting academic knowledge is very effective, more effective perhaps than the American way because a firm can more easily identify the management difficulty, assemble the problem-solving team, and effect a solution than can a business school. The firm is closer to and more intimately involved with the problem (Locke interview, Koblenz, July 20, 1994).

Huchzermeier observes that the locus of German management is in the firm, not in the management profession itself, and the instrumentality Americans attach to it, the business school. The leadership locus also explains why German management attributes differ from American. German executives disregard, in Peter Lawrence's words, "the general process of communication, decision-making, coordinating and control" (Lawrence, 1980, 56), the sort of managerialism taught in American business schools, for the specialism of their actual work. To acquire the managerial attributes that Germans prize, they follow a different academic and career path. They focus on subject-based pre-experience education (law, business economics, and above all engineering) and do research projects at university. And in the firm they work in their specialism until promoted into higher echelons.

Locating the center of management gravity in the firm instead of in a management caste also conditions attitudes towards codetermination. The US management caste perceived it as a threat to management power; US business schools exclude a firm's nonmanagement employees from their programs. They are schools for a management caste. German firms can much more easily look on codetermination as a management opportunity, as Professor Wildemann explained in Chapter 3; academic consultants from faculties or institutes of business economics who implemented Japanese production techniques in German firms worked closely and successfully with members of the works councils and trade unions. German professors of business economics, moreover, because they do not work in American-style business schools, teach courses to employee representatives involved in codetermination. With slight modifications to account for cultural differences, the German experience of a firm-centered management also pertains in Japan. Management in both countries has been and is far too important to be left to business schools or a management caste, especially since in America they both have renounced any sense of responsibility towards the life of the community or towards promoting the sustainability of the firm on whose existence the community depends.

How about reform?

If managerialism and business school education foster a lack of balance in American life, what can be done to restore it? Opponents of reform usually base their defense on anti-statist principles. If they are willing to concede that markets do not function rationally all the time, they think that governments never do. And they can point to a raft of examples to prove their point – the most significant being the dismal failure of centrally planned and controlled command socialist economies. Rather than enter the labyrinth of this debate, which is largely sterile, our attention shifts to reform of civil society, meaning reforms that could help the interaction among interested parties within firms function fairly without the need for constant bureau-cratic state regulation and the intervention of state control mechanisms.

Need for reform, however, is not just a matter of fairness. A US mass consumption economy depends on the presence of a relatively affluent middle class to buy the products peddled on world markets. With less money, consumers after 1980 could only keep purchasing with borrowed money. Lenders in America have been ingenious in devising ways to increase middle-class indebtedness, namely through a lucrative credit card industry and the creation of the subprime sector in real estate mortgages. But the system has run out of gas. Cash-strapped Americans, unable to repay the loans, are increasingly driven into bankruptcy. The long-term solution to the credit crisis, then, depends to a great extent on the restoration of patterns of wealth sharing like those that emerged in the thirty years following World War Two. Economic prosperity with low unemployment depends on it.

Guidelines for reform

This book considers US managerialism to be a principal cause of wealth maldistribution and a chief promoter of bad manage-ment in finance and industry. To counter the effects of manage-rialism, the analysis the study presents points to a two-pronged reform. First, the position of management in nonfinancial firms must be strengthened in order to protect the firm-entity from outside predators operating out of investment banks and hedge funds. This could be accomplished by adopting a two-tier board system, like the German one, with supervisory boards elected by stakeholders protecting the firm-entity from hostile takeovers and buyouts. Some protection of the firm-entity could also be afforded by limiting the voting rights of institutional investors in matters of mergers and acquisitions and takeovers. In Germany most stockholders have limited voting rights in these matters. The statement on German Generally Accepted Management Principles, moreover, allows managing directors in the firm to carry out a "protective function" that stops shareholders from making "exaggerated demands" on the firm (von Werder and Grundel, 2001, 102).

Second, participation in the selection of CEOs and boards needs to be extended to all company stakeholders. Unlike in America, where corporate CEOs often preside over the board of directors, in Germany members of a company's managing board cannot sit on the firm's supervisory board, which sets managing board salaries (von Werder and Grundel, 2001, 103). In big firms the stakeholders could also participate in the election of a compensation committee on salaries and bonuses. With this reform, stakeholders could have a say in how salaries and bonuses are fixed in their firms. There is no guarantee that employee representatives sitting on these committees would curb the excessive claims on a firm's resources of stockholders and upper management, but surely so long as the purse strings remain legally in the hands of stockholders and de facto almost exclusively under management's control, no fair-minded pay redistribution will occur through institutions within civil society.

The proposed legislation would not require great expenditure in public funds that would occasion the creation of massive administrative infrastructure, or progressive taxation to redistribute wealth. Nor would it require government intervention to set or cap executive salaries in ham-fisted bureaucratic interventions. It would simply allow redistribution to occur within firms themselves by stockholders and stakeholders.

The thrust of business school reform needs to be two-pronged as well. First, business schools' educational programs should serve a broader spectrum of business and industrial needs. Schools have to re-establish contact with manufacturing that they lost during the Japanese manufacturing challenge in the 1980s. There was no need for the automobile and other established industries to suffer so much had the leadership cadres seriously studied and pushed for work process reforms like TQM, rather than, as in the business school case, mostly ignoring them. Efforts also have to be made in business schools to respond to the criticism of the post-autistic movement in economics, to make study programs reflect realities in practice, rather than the belief of economics and finance professors in the omniscience of their models.

The second prong of business school reform needs to take on managerialism. Business schools should not just serve a management caste but business and industrial firms as entities. Therefore, they must broaden contacts to all firm stakeholders, including members of trade unions and other nonmanagement employees (as, for example, in teaching courses to employee members of compensations committees). To justify their existence as public institutions, business schools must also be proactive in leading management back to social responsibility, or business schools (instead of arts and humanities programs in universities) should be shut down, since there is ample evidence of the harm they have done, and that other countries have prospered without them.

Can US business schools and the management caste carry through any meaningful reforms along the lines suggested? The answer is no. People in top business schools believe their propaganda; they – perhaps out of self-preservation and certainly out of self-promotion – have not grasped the idea that good management education can occur without business schools or that they should serve broader interests than those of the management caste. Witness the outlook of Harvard Business School's new dean, Nitin Nohria, whose recent leadership handbook promotes the connection between business schools and managerialism (Nohria and Khurana, 2010).

Nor can the US management caste be expected voluntarily to give up its power and wealth. To retain both is why control over executive pay is so important to the caste. Right now management is in the enviable position of setting its own salaries and bonuses, and it will fight in the US and the UK to retain this power and to spread it internationally to firms as members of a privileged worldwide executive club. Despite the outrageous spectacle of seeing executives receive huge payouts in failing companies, nothing has been done to stop it, except ineffectual jawboning.

Not much reform can be expected either from the political side of the American ledger. Out-of-balance America has developed into a conflicted society, demoralized, politically paralyzed, bankrupt, and despairing. There is little stomach in the country to raise taxes to avoid deficits, little stomach, on the other hand, to raise deficit spending in order to stimulate the economy; there is no stomach for a fight to take corporate money out of electoral politics, or to stop the lobbyists from writing the legislation Congress passes, or to halt the endless spending on war and armaments, or to reform seriously any level of the educational system. Americans are like transfixed rabbits caught in the glare of onrushing headlights – cynically preaching the saying *Enrichissez-vous*, the nineteenth-century French equivalent of Greed is Good, or repeating the *bon mot* that amused Louis XV's court, in a regime on its last legs: *Après nous le déluge!*

If people want a solution to the problems that managerialism and US business school education induce, do not look to America. Look outside the United States for impetus and remedy. In the 1990s that would have been impossible. After the fall of communism, the globalization of US managerial, market-driven financial capitalism took on new life. But the recent financial turmoil has turned into a eureka event in world history, where observers suddenly discovered that the emperor has no clothes. Yukio Hatoyama, just before he became Japanese prime minister, phrased it this way:

> The recent economic crisis resulted from a way of thinking based on the idea that American-style free market economics represented a universal and ideal economic order, and that all countries should modify their traditions and regulations governing their economies in line with global (or rather American) standards ... Our responsibility as politicians is to refocus our attention on those non-economic values that have been thrown aside by the march of globalism. We must work on policies that regenerate the ties that bring people together, that take greater account of nature and the environment, that rebuild welfare and medical systems, that provide better education and child-rearing support, and that address wealth disparities. (Hatoyama, 2009, 1–2)

Hatoyama is not a radical anti-American venting spleen against the Great Satan. Hardly any Japanese politician is, in a cautious country that still depends on the US for its economic security and military defense. His doubts, therefore, express a growing change in world opinion among moderates who have been shocked by American managerialism's wanton belief that greed is good and profit maximization is to be sought at all costs, even, if necessary, through what ordinary people would call swindle.

World political leaders defend their peoples from the machinations of incompetent and insensitive financial traders in America and Britain. This happened unilaterally recently in the German Bundestag's prohibition of the short selling of bonds, regionally in the euro zone countries' growing refusal to let their currency be ruined by speculators operating outside the euro zone, trading in currency markets located in London and

New York, and in Chinese and Japanese decisions to monitor exchange rates rather than leave them at the mercy of US- and UK-based currency dealers (Kaletsky, 2010). The attempt to introduce balance through multilateralism is also gaining ground in the press to expand international economic and financial groupings to include representatives from developing and emerging economies and in efforts to expand participation in the United Nations.

It is also happening in jurisdictions that have been the focus of this study. Probably to non-Americans the most upsetting feature of US managerialism and the US business school outlook is the disregard for the poor. Rich Americans enjoy bounty without responsibility because they have wide spaces to exploit. Distressed Americans have not had to be taken care of; they simply moved out, from the Rust Belt to the South and the Southwest, from the inner-city blight to suburbia, with attendant shopping malls. In China, with 1.2 billion people, 800 million of whom are extremely poor peasants, the leadership has few demographic options – least of all because the country has a revolutionary past. That explains the emphasis there on a moral compass, described in Chapter 2.

The ethics of individualism might still resonate in America, although less convincingly than in the past, but it does not make much sense in a country such as China, where the leadership, and the middle classes, are sitting on top of a huge underclass that seeks freedom from want. The leadership class cannot dump its population on empty lands like American leaders; that is why Chinese leadership embraces a moral philosophy that promotes community values and a redistribution ethic. Chinese authorities turned to Kong Fuzi not to US individualism for their moral compass because they realize that China's leadership class cannot survive if it does not adhere to a broad distribution ethic and turn it enough into a reality to escape social breakdown.

Among the rapidly developing BRIC (Brazil, Russia, India, and China) countries, the Chinese government has taken the moral high ground by officially espousing policies that close the gap between the rich and poor and bring a balanced development between poorer and richer regions of the country. This is occurring elsewhere as well. In Brazil, people now call into question the American-sponsored administrative reforms, with the support of US-dominated agencies such as the IMF, that introduced global managerialism into many countries during the 1990s. In Brazil these reforms stressed "efficiency," and "the theories and practice of business management," in a new "managerialist state," meant to replace the old, inefficient, "developmentalist international state." The new managerialist state offered a "friendly and less contested context for the adoption of more liberal market-oriented policies, while retaining the power and authority of elite politicians and technocrats" (Imasato and Pieranti, 2010, no page numbers). Critics of this international managerialism nowadays dislike the "managerialist" state in Brazil, for the same reasons Prime Minister Hatoyama gave when condemning US freemarket-style economics in Japan – because it downgraded democratic participation and distracted government from its "societal roles."

To defend themselves from the charge of moral bankruptcy, the US management caste and their business school partners customarily switch the subject from ethics to economics – to the superiority of neoliberal market systems as compared to the economic failure of the socialist alternative. Although this might have made sense in the past, persistent US attacks on socialism today add up to beating a dead horse. Few in the developing non-Western world are interested in socialism. People everywhere in the Eurasian heartland are in fact busy dismantling socialism, by privatizing enterprises and opening up markets; they are engaged in a rapid expansion of international transportation systems, and in developing multinational trade at a remarkable pace. The building marvels of today are being erected outside America – while America fritters away its resources on lost wars at the cost of repairing its dilapidated infrastructure. The contrast between dynamic American capitalism and stagnant socialism only exists in misinformed American minds; reality now is a decaying US economic structure competing with a dynamic Eurasian continent, as every person who rides the bullet trains in Europe, China, South Korea, and Japan and visits recently constructed coordinated trade centers readily grasps.

Thus, the choice is not between socialism and unregulated US neoliberal market capitalism, but between the latter and an internationally regulated form of dynamic capitalism in which firms are more efficient because of participative management, and the markets function better because of a more equitable distribution of wealth in society. Unless a combination of domestic and international political pressures brings the necessary reforms to managerialism and business schools in the US, they will not be part of the solution to current woes but a continued cause of dislocation in American society and in the world economy.

References

"A Survey on Religion" (2007). *The Economist* (November 1). First print edition, 1–5.

Abegglen, J. and Stalk Jr., G. (1988). *Kaisha: The Japanese Corporation*. New York: Basic Books, Harper Collins.

Ackoff, R. (1979). "The Future of Operational Research is Past." *Journal of the Operational Research Society*, 30, 93–104.

Adams, J. (1995). "The 'British Disease' and the 'Japanization' of British Industry: Conjuncture or Continuity in World History." Master's thesis in History, University of Hawaii at Manoa, 1995.

Adams, T. and Smith, Y. (2010). "CDO Market – Rife with Collusion and Manipulation?" *Huffington Post* (April 23).

Albert, M. (1993). *Capitalism against Capitalism*. London: FWEW.

Alic, J. A., Branscomb, L., Brooks, H., and Carter, A. (1992). *Beyond Spinoff: Military and Commercial Technologies in a Changing World*. Boston, MA: Harvard Business School Press.

Amadae, S. M. (2003). *Rationalizing Capitalist Democracy: The Cold War Origins of Rational Choice Liberalism*. University of Chicago Press.

Amadae, S. M. and de Mesquita, B. B. (1999). "The Rochester School: The Origins of Positive Political Theory." *Annual Review of Political Science*, 2, 269–95.

Arrow, K. J. (1951). *Social Choice and Individual Values*. New York: Cowles Foundation Monograph.

Arrow, K. and Debreu, G. (1954). "Existence of a Competitive Equilibrium for a Competitive Economy." *Econometrica*, 22(3), 265–90.

Bach, G. L. (1958). "Some Observations on the Business School of Tomorrow." *Management Science*, 4(4) (July), 351–64.

Bainbridge, S. M. (1998). "Corporate Decision Making and the Moral Rights of Employees: Participatory Management and Natural Law." *Participatory Management* (September 28), 1–67.

Baldridge, V. J. (1971). *Power and Conflict in the University*. New York: John Wiley and Sons.

Bamberg, H.-D., Kröger, H.-J., and Kuhlmann, R. (eds.), (1979). *Hochschulen und Gewerkschaften: Erfahrungen, Analysen und Perspektiven*. Cologne: Gewerkschaftliche Kooperationspraxis.

Bátiz-Lazo, B., Müller, K., and Locke, R. R. (2008). "Transferring Rhineland Capitalism to the Polish–German Border." *International Journal of Bank Marketing*, 26 (2), 76–98.

Bell, D. (1951). "The Language of Labor." *Fortune* (September).

Bellah, R. N. (2000). "The True Scholar." *Academe, 86* (January and February), 1–10.

Berle, A. and Means, G. (1932). *The Modern Corporation and Private Property*. New York: Harcourt, Brace & World, Inc.

Berninger, E. H. (1974). *Otto Hahn*. Hamburg: Rowohlt Verlag.

Bernstein, J. M. (2010). "Hegel on Wall Street." Opinionator. *New York Times* (October 3).

Best, M. H. (2001). *The New Competitive Advantage: The Renewal of American Industry*. Oxford University Press.

Beyer, P. (2006). "Postmodernism and Religion." *Catholic Issues* website. Retrieved from http://home.adelphi.edu/-catissue/ARTICLES/BEYER96. HTM.

Bixby, R. E. (2002). "Solving Real-World Linear Programs: A Decade or More of Progress." *Operations Research*. 50(1), 3–15.

Bonder, S. (2002). "Army Operations Research – Historical Perspectives and Lessons Learned." *Operations Research* 50(1), 25–34.

Boole, G. (1854). *An Investigation of the Laws of Thought*. London: Walton & Maberly.

Borg, M. J. (1994). *Jesus in Contemporary Scholarship*. Valley Forge: Trinity Press International.

Bottom, W. P. (2009). "Organizing Intelligence: Development of Behavioral Science and the Research Based Model of Business." *Journal of the History of the Behaviorial Sciences* 45(3) (Summer), 253–83.

Bouée. C. (2010). *China's Management Revolution: Spirit, Land, Energy*. Basingstoke: Macmillan.

Bowley, G. (2011). "The New Speed of Money, Reshaping Markets." Business Day, *New York Times* (January 1), 1–4.

Brignall, M. (2004). "Set Course: Islamic Management, Banking and Finance." *Guardian.* (July 3). Retrieved from http://www.guardian.co.uk/money/2004/jul/03/careers.postgraduate?INTCMP=SRCH.

Burnham, J. (1937). *The Managerial Revolution: What Is Happening in the World.* New York: John Day Co.

Burton, K. (2005). "Cover Story: Griffin's Citadel." *Bloomberg's Market* (June), 1–7.

Capra, F. (1982). *The Turning Point: Science, Society, and the Rising Culture.* New York: Simon & Schuster.

Carew, A. (1987). *Labour under the Marshall Plan: The Politics of Productivity and the Marketing of Management Science.* University of Manchester Press.

Castells, M. and Hall, P. (1994). *Technopoles of the World: The Making of Twenty-First-Century Industrial Complexes.* London: Routledge.

Chan, S. (2010). "Academic Economists to Consider Ethics Code." Business Day, *New York Times* (December 31).

Chandler, A. D., Jr. and Redlich, F. (1961). "Recent Developments in American Business Administration and Their Conceptualization." *Business History Review*, 35(1), 1–27.

Chapman, G. (2004). *The Five Love Languages.* New York: Northfield Press.

Child, J. (1982). *Professionals in the Corporate World: Values, Interests and Control.* Birmingham: University of Aston Management Centre.

—— (2007). "Academic Freedom – The Threat from Managerialism." Paper presented at the Birmingham Workshops on Academic Freedom and Research/Learning Cultures.

Cobb, J. B., Jr. (1980). "A Critical View of Inherited Theology." *Christian Century* (February 20), 194–97.

—— (2007). "A Theology of Enjoyment for a Post Capitalist Life." Lecture 9, (July 17). St. Andrews Church, Vancouver, BC.

—— (2009a). "Capital." Address delivered at conference in Suzhou, China (January).

—— (2009b). "Religion and Economics." Presentation. Claremont Democratic Club. (May 8).

Collcutt, R. H. (1981). "OR Changes." *Journal of the Operational Research Society*, 32, 361–69.

Cooper, W. W. (2002). "Abraham Charnes and W. W. Cooper (et al.): A Brief History of a Long Collaboration in Developing Industrial Uses of Linear Programming." *Operations Research.* 50(1) (January–February), 35–41.

Cootner, P. (ed.). (1964). *The Random Character of Stock Market Prices.* Boston: MIT Press.

Croce, B. (1963). *History of Europe in the Nineteenth Century.* New York: Harcourt, Brace & World, Inc.

Crowell, T. (2005). "The Confucian Renaissance." *Asia Times* (November 16), 1–3.

Cummings, W. K. (1990). *Education and Equality in Japan.* Princeton University Press.

Cunliffe, A. L. (2009). "The Philosopher Leader: On Relationalism, Ethics and Reflexivity – A Critical Perspective to Teaching Leadership." *Management Learning*, 40(1) (February), 87–101.

Dando, M. R. and Bennett, P. G. (1981). "A Kuhnian Crisis in Management Science." *Journal of the Operational Research Society*, 32, 90–103.

de Gaulle, C. (1974). "Mobilisation économique à l'étranger." Reprinted in *Trois Études*. Paris: Plon.

Deming, W. E. (1982). *Quality, Productivity, and Competitive Position.* Boston: MIT CAES.

—— (1986). *Out of the Crisis.* Boston: MIT CAES.

Dobbin, F. and Jung, J. (2010). "The Misapplication of Mr. Michael Jensen: How Agency Theory Brought Down the Economy and Why It Might Again." In Lounsburg, M. and Hirsch, P. M. (eds.). *Markets on Trial: The Economic Sociology of the US Financial Crisis* (pp. 29–64). Bingley, UK: Emerald Group Publishing.

Dore, R. (2006). "Deviant or Different? Corporate Governance in Japan and Germany." *Corporate Governance*, 13(3) (May), 437–46.

Dorfman, J., Samuelson, P. and Solow, R. (1958). *Linear Programming and Economic Analysis.* New York: McGraw Hill.

Dörrenbächer, C. (2004). "Fleeing or Exporting the German Model? – the Internationalization of German Multinationals in the 1990s." *Competition and Change*, 8(4), 443–56.

Edwards, J. D. (1998). "Managerial Influences in Public Administration." *International Journal of Organization Theory and Behavior*, 1(4), 1–5.

Edwards, J. and Fischer, K. (1994). *Banks, Finance and Investment in Germany.* New York: Cambridge University Press.

Eliasson, G. (1998). "The Nature of Economic Change and Management in the Knowledge-Based Information Economy," Paper. KTH Stockholm Department of Industrial Management.

Engell, J. and Dangerfield, A. (1998). "The Market-Model University. Humanities in the Age of Money." *Harvard Magazine*. May/June, 12–53. Retrieved from http://harvardmagazine.com/1998/05/forum.html

Engwall, L. and Zamagni, V. (eds.) (1998). *Management Education in Historical Perspective.* Manchester University Press.

Enteman, W. F. (1993). *Managerialism: The Emergence of a New Ideology.* Madison: University of Wisconsin Press.

Fackler, A. (2006). "Japan Makes More Cars Elsewhere." *New York Times* (August 6).

Financial Modelers' Manifesto (2009). Paul Wilmott's Blog. Posted January 8, 2009.

Fish, S. (2010). "The Crisis of the Humanities Officially Arrives." *New York Times*. Retrieved from http://opinionator.blogs.nytimes.com/2010/10/11/the-crisis-of-the-humanities-officially-arrives/

Fortun, M. and Schweben, S. S. (1993). "Scientists and the Legacy of World War II: The Case of Operations Research." *Social Studies of Science* 23(4), 595–642.

Foster, R. N. and Kaplan, S. (2001). *Creative Destruction: Why Companies that Are Built to Last Underperform in the Market and How to Successfully Transform Them*. New York: McKiney & Company.

Fruin, M. W. (1992). *The Japanese Enterprise System: Competitive Strategies and Cooperative Structures*. New York: Oxford University Press.

Fruin, M. W. and Nishiguichi, T. (1993). "Supplying the Toyota Production System: Intercorporate Organization Evolution and Supplier Subsystems." In Kogut, B. (ed.). *Country Competitiveness: Technology and the Organizing of Work* (pp. 225–46). New York: Oxford University Press.

Fullbrook, E. (Ed.). (2003). *The Crisis in Economics: The Post-Autistic Economics Movement – The first 600 days*. London and New York: Routledge.

—— (2006). "Economics and Neo-liberalism." In Hassan, H. (2006). *After Blair: Politics after the New Labour Decade*. London: Lawrence & Wishart.

Gordon, R. A. and Howell, J. E. (1959). *Higher Education for Business*. New York: Columbia University Press.

Graves, A. P. (1993). *Global Competition and the European Automobile Industry: Opportunities and Challenges*. Cape Cod: IMUP.

Grey, C. (1996). "Towards a Critique of Managerialism: The Contribution of Simone Weil." *Journal of Management Studies*, 33(5), (September), 591–611.

Grudem, W. (2003). *Business for the Glory of God: The Bible's Teaching on the Moral Goodness of Business*. Minneapolis, MN: Crossway Books.

Gruening, G. (1998). "Origin and Theoretical Basis of the New Public Management (NPM)." Paper given to the IPMN Conference, Salem, OR (June).

Haley, K. B. (2002). "War and Peace: The First 25 Years of OR in Great Britain." *Operations Research*, 50 (2), (January–February), 82–88.

Hall, P. A and Thelen, K. (2009). "Institutional Change in Varieties of Capitalism." *Socio-Economic Review*, 7(1), 7–34.

Hall, R. W. (1993). *The Soul of Enterprise: Creating a Dynamic Vision for American Manufacturing*. New York: Harper Collins.

Haneef, M. and Amin, R. M. (2008). "Teaching Islamic Economics in Malaysian Universities: Lessons from the Department of Economics,

International Islamic University Malaysia (IIUM)." Paper presented at the 6th International Conference on Islamic Economics and Finance, Jakarta, and Islamic Economics Curriculum Workshop in Kuala Lumpur (August).

Harris. L. (2010). "Open Letter of Support for Philosophy at Howard University. Alain Locke Society." (November 18). Purdue University, Department of Philosophy. Retrieved from http://alainlocke.com/?p=56

Hart, D. (2007). "Leftward Christian Soldiers." *The American Conservative*, (January 29). Retrieved from http://amconmag.com/article/2007/jan/29/00024//

Hartmann, H. (1963). *Amerikanische Firmen in Deutschland: Beobachtungen über Kontakte und Kontraste zwischen Industriegesellschaften*. Westdeutscher Verlag.

Hatoyama, Y. (2009). "A New Path for Japan." Op-ed article, *New York Times* (August 27).

Hayashi, S. and Baldwin, F. (1989). *Culture and Management in Japan* (revised edn.). University of Tokyo Press.

Hofstede, G. H. (1978). "The Poverty of Management Control Philosophy." *Academy of Management Review*, 3(3), 450–61.

Homburg, H. (1978). "Anfänge des Taylorsystems in Deutschland vor dem Ersten Weltkrieg." *Geschichte und Gesellschaft* 4(2), 17–30.

Howson, A. G. (1978). "Change in Mathematics Education, since the Late 1950s, Great Britain." *Educational Studies in Mathematics* 9(2), 183–223.

Hudson, M. (2010). "The Use and Abuse of Mathematical Economics." *Real-World Economics Review* 54, December 17, 2–22.

Hughes, J. W. P. (2002). "Navy Operations Research." *Operations Research* 50(1), 103–111.

Ichbiah, D. and Knepper, S. L. (1992). *The Making of Microsoft: How Bill Gates and His Team Created the World's Most Successful Software Company*. Rocklin, CA: Prima Publishing.

Ichijo, K. and Nonaka, I. (eds.). (2007). *Knowledge Creation and Management: New Challenges for Managers*. New York: Oxford University Press.

Imasato, T., Martins, P. E. M., and Pieranti, O. P. (2010). "Administrative Reforms and Global Managerialism: A Critical Analysis of Three Brazilian State Reforms." *Canadian Journal of Administrative Science*. ASAC. John Wiley & Sons, Ltd., 1–15.

Ishikawa, K. (1985). *What is Total Quality Control? The Japanese Way* (translated by D. J. Lu). Englewood Cliffs: Prentice-Hall.

Jackson, G. and Moerke, A. (2005). "Continuity and Change in Corporate Governance: Comparing Germany and Japan." *Corporate Governance* 13(3) (May), 351–61.

Janis, I. L. (1972). *Victims of Group Think*. New York: Houghton Mifflin.

Jensen, M. C. and Smith, C. W. (1984). "The Theory of Corporate Finance: A Historical Overview." In Jensen, M. C. and Smith, C. W. (eds.). *The Modern Theory of Corporate Finance*. New York: McGraw Hill, 2–20.

Jeuck, J. E. (1973). "Business Education: Some Popular Models." *Library Quarterly* 43(4), (October), 281–92.

Johannson, K. and Weissbach, J. (1979). "Zusammenarbeit von Gewerkschaften und Hochschulen in der Weiterbildung." In H.-D. Bamberg, H.-J. Kröger and R. Kuhlmann, *Hochschulen und Gewerkschaften* (pp. 115–30). Cologne: Bund Verlag.

John, R. R. (1997). "Elaborations, Revisions, Dissent: Alfred D. Chandler Jr.'s *The Visible Hand* after Twenty Years." *Business History Review* 71(2), 151–200.

Johnson, H. T. (1978). "Management Accounting in an Early Multidivisional Organization: General Motors in the 1920s." *Business History Review* 52 (4) (Winter), 490–513.

—— (ed.). (1992). *Relevance Regained: From Top-Down Control to Bottom-Up Empowerment*. New York: Free Press.

—— (2010). "Toyota's Current Crisis: The Price of Focusing on Growth Not Quality." *Systems Thinker* 21(1), (February), 1–6.

Johnson, H. T. and Bröms, A. (2000). *Profit Beyond Measure: Extraordinary Results through Attention to Process and People*. Boston: Nicolas Breakley Publishing.

Johnson, H. T. and Kaplan, R. S. (1987). *Relevance Lost: The Rise and Fall of Management Accounting*. Boston: Harvard University Press.

Johnson, R. A. (2009). *Testimony of Robert A Johnson Before the US House of Representatives Committee on Financial Services* (1–26). (October 7). www.house.gov/apps/list/hearing/financialsves_dem_/raj_revisit_testi-mony.pdg

Kaletsky, A. (2010). "Blaming China won't Help the Economy." Op-ed contribution, *New York Times* (September 27). Retrieved from www.nytimes.com/2010/09/27/ioubuib.27kaletsky.html?_r=1&scp==Kaletsky&st=cse.

Kaplan, R. S. (1991). "Quality in Business School Education and Research." Paper presented to the Annual Meeting of the American Assembly of Collegiate Schools of Business, St. Louis, MO. (April 22).

Kenney, K. (1999). "Transplantation: A Comparison of Japanese Television Assembly Plants in Japan and the United States." In Liker, J. K., Fruin, W. M. and Adler, P. S. (eds.). (1999). *Remade in America: Transplanting and Transforming Japanese Management Systems* (pp. 256–93). New York: Oxford University Press.

Kenney, M. and Florida, R. (1993). *Beyond Mass Production: The Japanese System and Its Transfer to the US*. New York: Oxford University Press.

Khurana, R. (2007). *From Higher Aims to Hired Hands: The Social Transformation of American Business Schools and the Unfulfilled Promise of Management as a Profession*. Princeton University Press.

Kimball, B. A. (2009). *The Inception of Modern Professional Education, C. C. Langdell, 1826–1906*. University of North Carolina Press.

Klüber, F. (1977). *Arbeit, Mitbestimmung und Eigentum nach katholischer Soziallehre*. Regensburg University, Faculty of Catholic Theology. File name: 1977-08-a, pp. 495–566. Retrieved from http://library.fes.de/gmh/main/pdf-files/gmh/1977/1977-08-a0495.pdf

Koch, E. (1960). "Mathematik – pro und kontra." *Der Volkswirt* 12(24), 1176–78.

Korn, R. (2010). "Financial Mathematics: Between Stochastic Differential Equations and Financial Crisis." In Devroye, L., Karfasözen, B. Kohler, M. and Korn, R. (eds.). (2010). *Recent Developments in Applied Probability and Statistics* (pp. 223–28). New York: Physica Verlag.

Kosman, J. (2010). *The Buyout of America: How Private Equity Will Cause the Next Great Credit Crisis*. New York: Portfolio.

Kuran, T. (1997). "The Genesis of Islamic Economics: A Chapter in the Politics of Muslim Identity." *Social Research* 64(2), (Summer), 1–108.

Lane, C. (2004). "Institutional Transformation and System Change: Change in Corporate Governance of German Corporations." Sociological Series, No. 65. Vienna, Austria: Institute of Advanced Studies (IHS), (June), 1–33.

Larsfeld, M. (1959). "Mathématiques et sciences sociales." *Revue de l'Enseignement sociale* 3, 142–43.

Lawrence, P. (1980). *Managers and Management in West Germany*. London: Croon Helm.

Lequéret, P. (1982). *Le Budget de l'État: Préparation, Exécution, Contrôle*. Paris: Documentation Française.

Lerner, J. (1992). "The Mobility of Corporate Scientists and Engineers between Civil and Defense Activities: Implications for Economic Competitiveness in the Post Cold-War Era." *Defense and Peace Economics* 3(3), 229–42.

Lewis, M. (2010). *The Big Short: Inside the Doomsday Machine*. London: Allen Lane (Penguin).

Lewis, S. J. (1985). *Forgotten Legions: German Army Infantry Policy, 1918–1941*. New York: Praeger.

Liker, J. K., Fruin, W. M. and Adler, P. S. (1999). "Bringing Japanese Management Systems to the United States: Transplantation or Transformation?" In Liker, J. K., Fruin, W. M., and Adler, P. S. (eds.). (1999). *Remade in America: Transplanting and Transforming Japanese Management Systems* (pp. 3–38). New York: Oxford University Press.

Lilienthal, D. (1953). *Big Business: A New Era*. New York: Columbia University Press.

Litterer, J. A (1961). "Systematic Management: The Search for Order and Integration." *Business History Review* 35 (Spring), 461–76.

Little, J. D. C. (2002). "Philip M. Morse and the Beginnings." *Operations Research* 50(1), 146–48.

Locke, R. (2005). "Japan, Refutation of Neo-liberalism." *Post-Autistic Economics Review* 23 (March), 1–17.

Locke, R. R. (1984). *The End of the Practical Man*. Greenwich, CT: JAI Press.

—— (1989). *Management and Higher Education since 1940*. Cambridge University Press.

—— (1996). *The Collapse of the American Management Mystique*. Oxford University Press.

—— (1999). "French and German Managerial Systems Projected into the Military Events of May–June 1940." Public lecture, Queen's University, Belfast (October 16). Paper available from author.

—— (2000). "American Business School Education and the Revolution in Interactive Information Technology." In Jeffcutt, P. (ed.). (2004). *The Foundations of Management Knowledge* (pp. 66–82). London: Routledge.

—— (2008). "Comparing the German and American Systems. Roundtable on Business Education. A Consideration of Rakesh Khurana's *From Higher Aims to Hired Hands.*" *Business History Review*, 82(2), 336–42.

—— (2009). "Managerialism and the Demise of the Big Three." *Real-World Economics Review* 51 (December 1), 28–47.

—— and Schöne, K. (2004). *The Entrepreneurial Shift*. Cambridge University Press.

Lorwin, V. R. (1954). *The French Labor Movement*. Cambridge, MA: Harvard University Press.

Luo, Y. (2000). *Guanxi and Business*. Honolulu, HI: University of Hawaii Press. Asia-Pacific Business Series.

Lütz, S. (2000). *From Managed to Market Capitalism? German Finance in Transition*. Discussion Paper 00/2, Max Planck Institute, Cologne.

McClean, M., Harvey, C. and Press, J. (2007). "Managerialism and the Post-war Evolution of the French National Business System." *Business History* 49(4), (July), 531–51.

McCumber, J. (2001). *Time in the Ditch: American Philosophy and the McCarthy Era*. Evanston, IL: Northwestern University Press.

—— (2011). "The Stone: The Failure of Rational Choice Philosophy." Opinion, *New York Times* (June 19).

McGarvey, A. (2004). "Carter's Crusade: Jimmy Carter explains how the Christian right isn't Christian at all." *The American Prospect* (April 5). Retrieved from www.prospect.org/cs/articles?article=carters_crusade

McKibben, B. (2005). "The Christian Paradox: How a Faithful Nation Gets Jesus Wrong." *Harpers Magazine* (August). Retrieved from www.harpers.org/archive/2005/08/0080695.

Magee, J. F. (2002). "Operations Research at Arthur D. Little, Inc.: The Early Years." *Operations Research* 50(1), (February), 149–53.

Marschal, J. (1940). "Danger de la méthode mathématique." *Revue de l'économie politique* 54, 245–61.

Masuda Research Project Team for Japanese Systems. (1985). *Japanese Systems: An Alternative Civilization?* Masuda Foundation. Tokyo: Sekotakku Kabushiki Kaisha.

Mattessich, R. (1960). "Zu Ischbodins Kritik der mathematischen Methode." *Zeitschrift für betriebswirtschaftliche Forschung* 12, 55–56.

Melvin, S. (2007). "Yu Dan and China's Return to Confucius." *International Herald Tribune*, Culture (August) 29, 1–3

Merkel, A. (2005). "Das 'C' in Namen der CDU." *Frühjahrstagung des Politischen Clubs* (2005).

Mintzberg, H., Simons, R., and Basu, K. (2002). "Beyond Selfishness," *MIT Sloan Management Review* 44 (1), (Fall), 67–74.

Mitchell, L. E. (2007). *The Speculation Economy: How Finance Triumphed Over Industry*. San Francisco: Berrett-Koehler Publishers, Inc.

Mofid, K. (2005). "The Roots of Economics – and Why It Has Gone so Wrong." In Braybrook, M. and Mofid, K. (eds.). (2005). *Promoting the Common Good: Bringing Economics and Theology Together Again*. London: Shepheard-Walwyn.

Monaghan, P. (2003). "Taking on 'Rational Man.' Dissident Economists Fight for a Niche in the Discipline." *Chronicle of Higher Education* 49 (January 24).

Moore, Beth (2004). *Believing God*. New York: B & H Publishing Group.

Moores, K. and Steadman, G. T. (1986). "Comparative Viewpoints of Groups of Accountants. More on the Entity-Proprietary Debate." *Accounting, Organization and Society* 11(1), 19–34.

"More Taiwanese Students Flock to Mainland to Further Studies." (2002). *China News Digest International, Inc.* (January 25). Retrieved from www.hartford-hwp.com/archives/55/640.html.

Munnell, A. H., Aubry, J.-P. and Muldoon, D. (2008). "The Financial Crisis and Private Defined Benefit Plans." Boston MA: *Center for Retirement Research at Boston College* 8 (November 18).

Nohria, N. and Khurana, R. (eds.). (2010). *Handbook of Leadership Theory and Practice: A Harvard Business School Centennial Colloquium*. Boston, MA: Harvard Business School Press.

Nonaka, I. and Takeuchi, H. (1995). *The Knowledge-Creating Company: How Japanese Companies Create The Dynamics of Innovation*. New York: Oxford University Press.

Orwell, G. (1997). *Animal Farm*. New York: Barnes & Noble.

Osteen, J. (2005). *Your Best Life Now*. New York: Simon & Schuster.

Page, T. (1952). "The Founding Meeting of the Operations Research Society." *Journal of the Operations Research Society* 1(1), 1–26.

Patterson, S. (2010). *The Quants: How a Small Band of Maths Wizards Took over Wall Street and Nearly Destroyed It*. New York: Randon House Business Books.

PEW Research Center for the People and the Press. (2002). "Americans Struggle with Religion's Role at Home and Abroad." *PEW Survey Report (2002). Faith Based Funding Backed, but Church–State Doubts Abound*. Retrieved from http://people-press.org/report/?pageid=112

Pierson, F. and Finberg, B. D. (1959). *The Education of American Businessmen: A Study of University-College Programs for Business Administration*. New York, Toronto and London: McGraw-Hill, Inc.

Piettre, A. (1961). "Économie et mathématiques." *Économie et humanisme* 20, 3–16.

Pil, F. K. and MacDuffie, J. P. (1999). "Transferring Competitive Advantage Across Borders: A Study of Japanese Auto Transplants in North America." In Liker, J. K., Fruin, W. M. and Adler. P. S. (eds.). *Remade in America*: *Transplanting and Transforming Japanese Management Systems* (pp. 39–74). New York: Oxford University Press.

Porter, M. (2007). "Doing Well at Doing Good: Do You Have a Strategy?" Paper presented at Willow Creek Association Leadership Summit. South Barrington, Illinois (August 10).

Preiss, H. (1979). "Gewerkschaften und Erziehung." In Bamberg, H.-D., Kröger, H.-J. and Kuhlmann, R. (eds.). (1979). *Hochschulen und Gewerkschaften* (pp. 501–03). Cologne: Bund Verlag.

Quiggin, J. (2003). "Word for Wednesday: 'managerialism (definition)." *Commentary* (July 2). Retrieved from http://johnquiggin.com/index.php/

Rasmus, J. (2004). *Pension Plans in the Corporate Cross-Hairs*. Kylos Productions. Retrieved from www.Kylosproductions.com/articles/pensions.html 1–5.

"Real Say on Pay." (2010). Editorial, *New York Times* (September 2).

Reich, R. B. (1992). *The Work of Nations: Preparing Ourselves for 21st Century Capitalism*. New York: Vintage Books.

Reynolds, P. D., Camp, S. M., Bygrave, W. D., Autio, E., and Hay, M. (2001). "2001 Executive Report". *Global Entrepreneurship Monitor*.

Reynolds, P. D., Storey, D. J. and Westhead, P. (1994). "Cross-national Comparisons of the Variation in New Firm Formation Rates." *Regional Studies* 28(4), 443–56.

Rheingold, H. (1991). *Virtual Reality*. New York: Summit Books.

Riedler, A. (1894). *Ein Rückblick auf die Weltausstellung in Chicago*. Berlin: THU.

Rivett, P. (1974). "Perspectives for Operational Research." *OMEGA* 2(2), 225–33.

—— (1981). "In Praise of Unicorns." *Journal of the Operational Research Society* 32, 1051–59.

Rosenzweig, P. (2010). "Robert S. McNamara and the Evolution of Modern Management." *Harvard Business Review* (December), 84–93.

Rother, M. (2010). *Toyota Kata: Managing People for Improvement, Adaptiveness and Superior Results*. New York: McGraw-Hill.

Sartre, J.-P. (1948). *Situations*. Paris: Plon.

Sass, S. A. (1982). *The Pragmatic Imagination: A History of the Wharton School, 1881–1981*. Philadelphia, PA: University of Pennsylvania Press.

Saxenian, A. (1994). *Regional Advantages*. Cambridge, MA: Harvard University Press.

—— (2000). "Networks of Immigrant Entrepreneurs." In Lee, C.-M., Miller, W., Gong-Hancock, M., and Rowan, S. (eds.). *The Silicon Valley Edge: A Habitat for Innovation and Entrepreneurship* (pp. 248–75). Stanford University Press.

Schifferes, S. (2007). "The Decline of Detroit." *Globalisation Reporter*, BBC News (July 1). Retrieved from http://news.bbc.co.uk/2/hi/business/6346299.stm

Schlesinger, L. and Mellado, J. (1991). "Willow Creek Community Church." Case study, *Harvard Business Review* (June 18). Prod no. 691102-HCB-ENG.

Schlossman, S., Sedlak, M. and Wechsler, H. (1987). *The "New Look": The Ford Foundation and the Revolution in Business Education*. Graduate Council Admission. Council Papers, Los Angeles, 1–17, 54–96.

Schmohl, J. (2009). "Entrepreneurial Exit Management – Key Success Factors of the Private Equity Buyout Options." PhD thesis no. 3792. University of St. Gallen, Graduate School of Business Adminstration (HSG) (October 19).

Schweikert, D. (2005). "You Can't Get There From Here: Reflections on 'Beijing Consensus.'" Paper for the International Symposium on the "China Model or Beijing Consensus for Development," Tianjin Normal University, Tianjin, China. (August 8). Retrieved from http://homepages.luc.edu/-dschwei/beijingconsensus.htm.

Sculley, J. (1987). *Odyssey: Pepsi to Apple: A Journey of Adventure, Ideas and the Future*. New York: Harper and Row.

Senge, P. M. (1990). *The Fifth Discipline: The Art and Practice of the Learning Organization*. New York: Doubleday.

—— (2000). "Foreword." In Johnson, H. T. and Bröms, A. (2000). *Profit Beyond Measure: Extraordinary Results Through Attention to Work and to People* (pp. ix–xvi). New York: Free Press.

Shad, J. S. R. (1984). "The Leveraging of America." *Security Exchange Commission News*. Washington, DC: (June 7), 1–7.

Sheard, P. (1994). "Interlocking Shareholdings and Corporate Governance." In Aoki, M. and Dore, R. (eds.). (1994). *The Japanese Firm: The Sources of Competitive Strength* (pp. 310-349). Oxford University Press.

Simon, H. (1996). *Hidden Champions: Lessons from 500 of the World's Best Unknown Companies*. Boston: Harvard Business School Press.

Smith, H. (1958). *The Religions of Man*. New York: HarperCollins.

Speidel, F. (2002). *Co-managed vs. Management-dominated Globalization: The Implication of Globalization on Industrial Relations in the German and French Car Industry with Particular Reference to the Cases of Volkswagen and Renault*. FiAB, Institut an der Ruhr-Universität Bochum. Arbeitspapier Nr. 2 ISSN 16120-1162, 2002.

Spender, J.-C. (2005). "Speaking about Management Education: Some History of the Search for Academic Legitimacy and the Ownership and Control of Management Knowledge." *Management Decision* 43(10), 1282-92.

—— (2007). "Management as a Regulated Profession: An Essay." *Journal of Management Inquiry* 16(1), 32-42.

—— (2008a). "Review: *From Higher Aims to Hired Hands* by Rakesh Khurana, Princeton NJ: Princeton University Press 2007." *Academy of Management Review* 33(4), 1022-26.

—— (2008b). "Can Simon's Notion of 'Bounded Rationality' Give Us New Ideas About Leadership?" *Leadership* 4, 95-109.

—— (2008c). "Organizational Learning and Knowledge Management: Whence and Whither?" *Management Learning* 39(2), 159-76.

Steger, W. A. (1979). "Assessment of Fifteen Years of Urban Modeling." *OMEGA* 7(6), 545-51.

Streeck, W. (1984). *Industrial Relations in West Germany: A Case Study of the Car Industry*. New York: St. Martin's.

Streeck, W. and Yamamura, K. (2001). *The Origins of NonLiberal Capitalism: Germany and Japan in Comparison*. Ithaca, NY: Cornell University Press.

Swatos, W. H. Jr. and Christianos, K. J. (1991). "Secularization Theory: The Cause of a Concept." *Sociology of Religion* (Fall), 1-15.

Taleb, N. N. (2001). *Fooled by Randomness: The Hidden Role of Chance in Life and in the Markets* (2nd edn.). New York: Random House.

—— (2010). "Did the Nobel Prize Help Trigger the Worst Financial Crisis Since the Great Depression?" *Reuters*. Stockholm (September 28). Retrieved from http://www.reuters.com/article/2010/09/28/us-nobel-crisis-interview-idUSTRE68R2SK20100928

Taylor, F. W. (1903). *Shop Management*. Transactions of the American Society of Mechanical Engineers XXIV.

—— (1911). *The Principles of Scientific Management*. New York: Harpers & Brothers.

Tobin, N. R., Ripley, K., and Teather, W. (1980). "The Changing Role of OR." *Journal of the Operational Research Society* 31(4), 279–88.

Tsutsui, W. (1998). *Manufacturing Ideology: Scientific Management in 20th Century Japan.* Princetion University Press.

Vagts, A. (1937). *A History of Militarism: Romance and Realities of a Profession.* New York: Norton.

Vaubel, L. (1952). *Unternehmer gehen zur Schule – Ein Erfahrungsbericht aus USA.* Düsseldorf: Droste.

Vernohr, B. and Meyer, K. E. (2007). "The German Miracle Keeps Running: How Germany's Hidden Champions Stay Ahead in the Global Economy." *Institute of Management,* Berlin School of Economics (March).

Vico, G. (2000). *New Science* (translated by A. Grafton and D. Marsh, 3rd edn.). New York: Penguin.

Vogel, S. K. (2006). *Japan Remodeled: How Government and Industry Are Reforming Japanese Capitalism.* Ithaca, NY: Cornell University Press.

Vogt, W. (1979). "Erich Schneider und die Wirtschaftstheorie," in *E. Schneider, 1900-1979, Gedenkband und Bibliographie* (pp. 13–48). (1980). Kiel, Germany: Kiel Institut für Weltwirtschaft an der Universität.

von Neumann, J. and Morgenstern, O. (1944). *Theory of Games and Economic Behavior.* Princeton University Press.

Walsh, M. W. (2005). "Whoops! There Goes Another Pension Plan." *New York Times* (October 15).

Waring, S. (1995). "Cold Calculus: The Cold War and Operations Research." *Radical History Review* 63, 28–51.

Werder, A. von, and Grundel, J. (2001). "Generally Accepted Management Principles (GAMP) – Functions, First Proposals, and Acceptance Among German Top Managers." *Corporate Governance* 9(2), (April), 101–09.

Wertz, M. (1993). "Wilhelm von Humboldt's Classical Education Curriculum." *The American Almanac* (1–7). (March 15). Retrieved from http://american_almanac.tripod.com/von humboldt.htm

Westney, E. (1987). *Imitation and Innovation: The Transfer of Western Organization Patterns to Meiji Japan.* Cambridge, MA: Harvard University Press.

Wesner, F. (2005). "Soziale Sicherung in der VR China: Bestandsaufnahme und Perspektiven." *Friedrich Ebert Stiftung.* Im Auftrag des Pekinger Büros, unter der Leitung von Roland Feicht, Peking (December).

Whitley, R. (1986). "The Transformation of Business Finance into Financial Economics: The Role of Academic Expansion and Changes in US Capital Markets." *Accounting, Organization and Society.* 11(2), 171–92.

Wolfe, A. (2004). "The Revival of Religion in America." *Chronicle of Higher Education* (October 22), 100–103.

Womack,J. P.,Jones, D. T. and Roos, D. (1990). *The Machine that Changed the World.* New York: Rawson Associates.

Yamashine, H. (1991). "Time and Innovation: The View from Japan." Stockton Lecture, London Business School.

Yasumuro, K. (1993). "Engineers as Functional Alternatives to Entrepreneurs in Japanese Industrialization." In Brown, J. and Rose, M. (eds.) (1993). *Entrepreneurship, Networks and Modern Business* (pp. 76–101). Manchester: Manchester University Press.

Yeh, K. (2007). "Taiwanese Students Flock to China in Search of Better Prospects." *Channel News Asia.* Retrieved from www.channelnews.asia. com/story285469/1/html

Zigarelli, M. (2008). *Management by Proverbs.* Longwood, FL: Xulon Press.

Zimmerman, R. J. (1982). "Trends and New Approaches in European Operational Research." *Journal of the Operational Research Society* 33, 597–603.

Index

About Zed Books

Zed Books is a critical and dynamic publisher, committed to increasing awareness of important international issues and to promoting diversity, alternative voices and progressive social change. We publish on politics, development, gender, the environment and economics for a global audience of students, academics, activists and general readers. Run as a co-operative, Zed Books aims to operate in an ethical and environmentally sustainable way.

Find out more at:
www.zedbooks.co.uk

For up-to-date news, articles, reviews and events information visit:
http://zed-books.blogspot.com

To subscribe to the monthly Zed Books e-newsletter, send an email headed 'subscribe' to
marketing@zedbooks.net

We can also be found on
Facebook, ZNet, Twitter and **Library Thing**.

CPSIA information can be obtained
at www.ICGtesting.com
Printed in the USA
LVHW040749080621
689671LV00004B/238